Ukraine

Second Edition

Ukraine

Second Edition

STEVEN OTFINOSKI

®

Facts On File, Inc.

Nations in Transition: Ukraine, Second Edition

Facts On File, Inc.
132 West 31st Street
New York NY 10001

Library of Congress Cataloging-in-Publication Data

Otfinoski, Steven.
    Ukraine / Steven Otfinoski.—Second Edition
        p. cm.—(Nations in transition)
    Includes bibliographical references and index.
    ISBN 0-8160-5115-1 (hc)
    1. Ukraine—Juvenile literature. I. Title. II. Series.

DK508.515.O88 2004
947.7—dc22   2004043241

Facts On File books are available at special discounts when purchased in bulk quantities for businesses, associations, institutions, or sales promotions. Please call our Special Sales Department in New York at (212) 967-8800 or (800) 322-8755.

You can find Facts On File on the World Wide Web at http://www.factsonfile.com

Text design by Erika K. Arroyo
Cover design by Nora Wertz
Maps by Sholto Ainslie

Printed in the United States of America

MP FOF 10 9 8 7 6 5 4 3 2 1

This book is printed on acid-free paper.

Contents

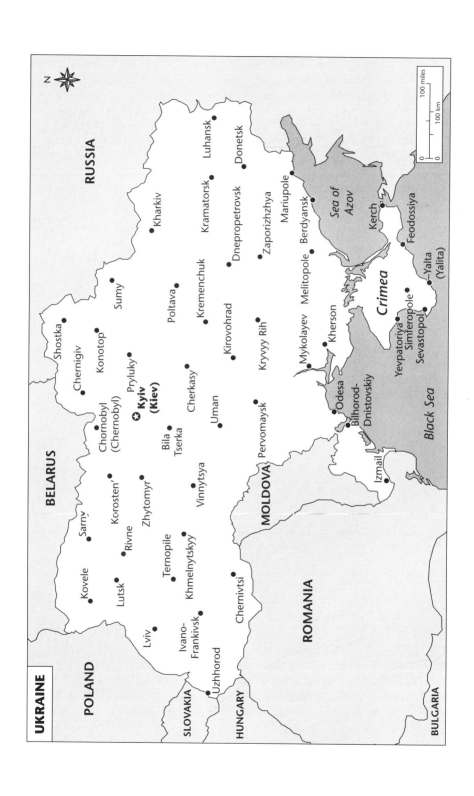

INTRODUCTION

On August 24, 2001, the republic of Ukraine celebrated the 10th anniversary of its independence from the Soviet Union. While this may not seem a major landmark for many countries—even those that like Ukraine, lived for decades under communism—it was a very special occasion in Ukraine. Those 10 years of freedom were, remarkably, the longest period of independence the country has ever known.

Long before it was incorporated into the Soviet Union, Ukraine had been dominated by foreign powers—primarily Poland and Russia. Until the 19th century, it was called "the Ukraine," referring to a region or area, rather than a nation of people with a common purpose. "Without a Ukrainian state, Ukrainian history was handed down as a footnote, considered no more than a provincial expression of the dominant power," notes Ukrainian-American writer Linda Hodges.

But no matter how others viewed them, the Ukrainians always considered themselves a nation—one with a unique culture and civilization. Ironically, that civilization gave birth to Russian civilization, which was first centered in the legendary city of Kyiv, Ukraine's capital city, better known in the West as Kiev.

The glory of Kyivan Rus, as the city-state came to be called, eventually gave way to Muscovy, centered around the city of Moscow to the north. The center of Slavic power shifted, never to return, and Ukraine, which means "borderland" in Russian, was a prize to be captured by one invading power after another. For the Russians it was a vast breadbasket, producing enough grain to feed much of the Russian Empire and, later, the Soviet Union. Its mines, factories, and industrial centers were equally important to those who controlled them.

Because of its importance, Ukraine was at times given a little more freedom than the other Soviet republics. Other times it was punished severely for its spirit of independence. Twice in the 20th century, it suffered horrendous famines and world wars in which millions of its people perished.

Today, Ukraine is facing another war, a war against itself. The ghost of the Soviet years haunts Ukraine and has led it down a dark road of repression, corruption, and bitter factionalism. Its standing in the international community has become so tarnished that soon after the 10th anniversary a group of businessmen founded Ukraine Cognita, an organization whose goal is to improve Ukraine's image abroad. Its first action was to commission a groundbreaking six-month study by two Austrian firms to find out what other countries thought of Ukraine. People from all walks of life in 19 countries were questioned in this massive study.

The results were unsettling. About 80 percent of the people interviewed thought Ukraine's image as bad as any in the world. Sixty percent believed Ukraine does not respect human rights, and 44 percent considered Ukraine politically unstable. The only areas in which respondents were positive about the country were agriculture, industry, sports, and culture.

Interestingly, more than 80 percent agreed that people in the West know too little about Ukraine. Ukraine Cognita is working to implement the study's recommendations, which include disseminating positive information, attracting foreign investors and tourists, and inviting foreign journalists to visit. In fall 2002, the group took 25 foreign journalists on a tour of the nation.

But even Ukraine Cognita realizes that marketing the country will be a hard sell. "The image of the country is of a totalitarian regime, no freedom of the press, no human rights, high corruption," admitted Ukraine Cognita's director Irina Gagarian. "It's a pity for a generation of Ukrainians, which is actually ready to make the country better for the future."

Many Ukrainians hope that the future is better than the last 10 years have been. Independence was anticipated as a time of great expansion and growth; instead, Ukraine's vast potential seemed to go to waste.

"When the Soviet Union disintegrated, Ukraine was expected to be the leading country," noted one Western investor. "Unfortunately, it did not work out that way." But before examining the way it *did* work out and why, a look at the land itself and its vast resources is needed.

Vast Steppes and Mighty Rivers

Ukraine was the second largest republic in the Soviet Union and one of the richest. Today, it is the largest nation completely located in Europe. Slightly smaller than the state of Texas, Ukraine covers 233,090 square miles (603,700 sq km). Geographically, Ukraine is at the very center of the Eurasian landmass. It is bordered on the north by Belarus and Russia; on the east by Russia; on the west by Hungary, Slovakia, and Poland; and on the south by the Black Sea, the Sea of Azov, Romania, and Moldova, another former Soviet republic.

Similar to Poland, Ukraine is primarily a flat country of vast plains, called steppes, and plateaus. There are only two mountain ranges in the country—the Carpathian Mountains in the west and the smaller

---

THE STEPPES—UKRAINE'S HEARTLAND

Any American from the Great Plains might feel right at home on the expansive southern steppes of Ukraine. Both these land regions are what agriculturists call "tillable steppes": flat, treeless grasslands with rich, fertile soil.

Ukraine's steppes are part of a vast plain that stretches from southern Ukraine into central Asia. While the Asian steppes are arid and desertlike, the more temperate Ukrainian steppes are still subject to cold winters and hot summers. When a summer drought strikes, it not only withers crops but sends strong hot winds that blow away the plowed earth, causing serious soil erosion. This happened in Ukraine on a tragic scale during the famine of 1946.

The Ukrainians love their steppes with a passion similar to what many Americans feel about the western prairie. Just as cowboys are associated with the prairie, so the colorful Kozaks, 17th-century patriotic warriors, are inextricably linked with the steppes they once roamed.

The Kozaks are long gone, but the steppes still hold a fascination for the farmers who daily till its soil. In the words of one American travel writer, the steppes are "wide as forever, [the] horizon blotted by nothing bigger than a haystack. In eastern parts one looks in vain for a hill while standing in what seems a tranquil sea of . . . black earth."

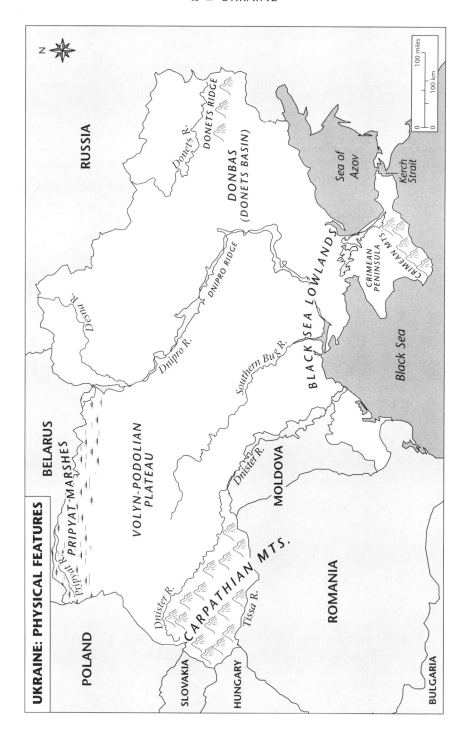

UKRAINE: PHYSICAL FEATURES

Crimean Mountains in the south. Mount Hoverla, the country's highest point at 6,764 feet (2,062 m), is in the Carpathians.

While Ukraine has few lakes, it is riddled with rivers and streams, more than 20,000 of them. There are four major rivers that divide the country from north to south. The largest is the Dnipro, the third longest river in Europe after the Volga and the Danube. It enters the country north from Belarus above Kyiv and makes its way eastward, dividing the country in two unequal halves. The Dnipro empties into the Black Sea near the city of Mykolayev. Navigable three seasons out of four, it has been a major trade route for centuries. The Dnister, which is impossible to navigate, rises in the west from the Carpathians and also empties into the Black Sea. The Donets runs across eastern Ukraine, while the Southern Bug is the only major river that starts and ends within Ukraine.

If the country were divided north to south into thirds, the northern third would be wooded and swampy; the central third, steppes covered with forest land; and the southern third, treeless steppes with black earth called *chernozem*, one of the most fertile soils on earth. Because of its size, Ukraine has a varied climate. Western Ukraine is milder in the winter

Rivers have been the lifeblood of Ukraine for centuries. Here the Dnipro River flows by the city of Kyiv and one of its oldest districts, the port of Podil.
(Courtesy Library of Congress)

than eastern Ukraine, but cooler in the summer. The climate in the far south is Mediterranean. Precipitation is much higher in the north than in the south.

A Proud People

Ukraine has a population of 48,055,439 (2003 estimate). Among the former republics, only Russia has more people. Nearly 78 percent of the population are ethnic Ukrainians, forming a distinct Slavic group. Russians make up about 17 percent of the population.

The remaining 5 percent are mostly Belarusan, Moldovan, Crimean Tatar, Bulgarian, Romanian, Polish, Jewish, or Hungarian. Centuries of war and strife have caused many Ukrainians to leave their homeland in pursuit of a better life. Some 12 million Ukrainians live in other ex-Soviet republics, including Russia. Another 4 million live in other countries—primarily Europe, the United States, and Canada.

Whether they live in their country or outside it, Ukrainians are a proud people—proud of their rich heritage and culture, proud of their ability to survive invaders and catastrophes. After centuries of having their identity suppressed, they are now reveling in it. They have stripped their maps of Russian names and replaced them with Ukrainian ones. The Ukrainian language, along with Ukrainian culture, art, and literature, is taught in schools throughout the country. Ukrainian folkways and traditional customs are followed religiously by millions.

But not everyone thinks independence is the greatest thing for Ukraine. "We were strong when we were the Soviet Union," says a Russian woman living in Donetsk, an industrial city and a Russian stronghold. "But now we don't amount to anything."

This judgment may be harsh but it is realistic. Promised reforms have been held back by a lack of freedom, corruption, and a failing economy. Transition, even after 10 years of independence, will not be easy, but then little has been easy for the Ukrainians, as their history readily testifies.

NOTES

p. vii "'Without a Ukrainian state . . .'" Linda Hodges and George Chumak, *Language and Travel Guide to Ukraine* (New York: Hippocrene Books, 1994), p. 2.

p. viii　"'The image of the country . . .'" *New York Times*, January 13, 2002, p. 3.

p. viii　"'When the Soviet Union . . .'" *Calgary Herald*, August 14, 1996, p. D8. CD NewsBank.

p. ix　"'wide as forever . . .'" Mike Edwards, "Ukraine," *National Geographic*, May 1987, p. 608.

p. xii　"'We were strong when we . . .'" Mike Edwards, "Ukraine: Running on Empty," *National Geographic*, March 1993, pp. 47–48.

PART I
History

ONE LAND, MANY MASTERS (PREHISTORY TO 1922)

It is not difficult to understand why many Russians feel that Ukraine should have remained a part of their nation after the breakup of the Soviet Union. It was here in the city-state of Kyiv that Russian civilization was first born around A.D. 800. But human history in Ukraine began long before that.

Archaeologists estimate that early people were living in the region as far back as 150,000 B.C. For thousands of years, these peoples were nomadic hunters. By about 4000 B.C., a people called Trypillians had cultivated crops and were living in crude villages. Little is known of the Trypillians other than that they lived in clan groups, built rectangular log houses, and made fine pottery.

More nomadic warrior groups started to migrate into the flat steppes of present-day Ukraine by about 1000 B.C. Among the first were the Cimmerians, who entered the Crimean area of southern Ukraine. They were driven into present-day eastern Turkey by the more savage Scythians around 700 B.C. The Scythians dominated Ukraine for the next 500 years, setting up a noble ruling class.

By about A.D. 500, various Slavic tribes, wandering the land in the wake of the Scythians, settled in southern Ukraine near the Black Sea. There they were safe from the warlike Huns of central Asia. Superb warriors themselves, these Slavs had begun to invade the Scythians' land about A.D. 300. Into this confusing mix entered the people who would succeed in unifying the Slavs into one people: the Varangians, or as the Slavs called them, the Rus. The Rus were actually Vikings, probably from Denmark, and were led by the great warrior Rurik. Rurik set up his headquarters in the city of Novgorod (in present-day western Russia). After his death in about 879, his successors founded a city to the south that was a more strategic center for their operation: Kyiv.

The Rise of Kyivan Rus

More than a city, Kyiv was a city-state, similar to those of ancient Greece, whose influence extended far beyond city walls. As Russian historian V. O. Kluchevsky states, Kyivan Rus was clearly "the birthplace of Russian nationality." In fact, although most Ukrainians call it Kyivan Rus, contemporary Russians prefer the term Kyivan Russia, linking the Kyiv city-state directly to the Russian Empire that later grew up around the city of Moscow.

By whatever name it is known, Kyiv quickly became one of the largest powers in medieval Europe. Located on the western banks of the Dnipro River, it was a major trading center between northern Europe and the Byzantine Empire to the south. Under the seventh ruler of the Rurik dynasty, Volodymyr the Great (see boxed biography) the Kyiv city-state entered its "golden age." A pagan, like his ancestors, Volodymyr converted to Christianity in 987. Christianity was becoming the chosen religion of kings and princes throughout Europe. Volodymyr saw Christianity as a means to unifying all the people of his kingdom into one powerful state.

Before converting, the king sent messengers to observe both the Roman Catholic and the Orthodox Byzantine branches of the Christian church.* Less impressed by the rites of the Roman church, the messengers had this to say about the services they attended at the (Orthodox) Cathedral of Hagia Sophia in Constantinople: "We knew not whether we were in heaven or on earth. For on earth there is no such splendor or such beauty, and we are at a loss to describe it."

---

*Due to differences regarding dogma and politics, the Christian church split in 1054.

VOLODYMYR THE GREAT (REIGNED 980–1015)

Everything about Volodymyr I of Kyiv was bigger than life. Terrible tyrant, brilliant administrator, stalwart soldier—he was all these things. He began his reign as a pagan, with at least seven wives, who fiercely persecuted Christians and other religious peoples. He later converted to Christianity and spread the faith among his subjects, applying the same zeal with which he had previously persecuted it.

Volodymyr's conversion may well have been more political than spiritual. After becoming a Christian, he married Anna, the sister of the Byzantine emperor Basil I, thus linking his kingdom with the greatest in the Eastern world. He strategically steered his children into marriages with the children of the kings and queens of several European powers.

Volodymyr turned Kyiv into a mighty fortress, safe from the many invaders who had plundered it regularly. Later, he transformed Kyiv into a center of culture and learning, building schools, libraries, and ornate churches.

As a soldier, he won back lands taken by the Poles to the west and defeated the Lithuanians, a threat from the north. By 1000, after 20 years of his rule, Kyivan Rus was the second largest empire in Europe. Only the Holy Roman Empire was bigger.

When Volodymyr was an old man, his son, Yaroslav, rebelled against him. After Volodymyr's death, his sons fought one another for 20 years to determine who would succeed him. Yaroslav finally emerged the victor. He proved to be a strong leader and truly his father's son. As for Volodymyr the Great, the Ukrainian Orthodox Church made this former pagan a saint.

Volodymyr was impressed by their report and chose the Orthodox Church, aligning himself with Byzantium, which became a powerful ally of Kyivan Rus for centuries to come. Volodymyr built churches, oversaw the conversion of all his subjects, forcibly if necessary, and built a state that would develop further under the rule of his son, Yaroslav the Wise (978–1054). Yaroslav promoted the arts, built towns, and created a system of laws to govern by. Under him, Kyiv's population rose to 80,000, making it as large as Paris, the biggest city in Western Europe at that time.

Volodymyr I, seen on this ancient banner with his minions, well deserved the title "the Great." He built Kyivan Rus into the second largest empire in Europe by the year 1000. (Courtesy Free Library of Philadelphia)

Kyiv was far more progressive than European cities. The peasantry was free and not bound to the land as under the feudal system in most European countries. Towns had democratic assemblies, or *veches,* which were open to all free men, although their decisions had to be unanimous.

But even at the height of Kyiv's greatness, fortunes began to shift. The flat steppes tempted yet another invader from the east, the Polovtsi, who were driven back by Manomekh, Yaroslav's grandson. The leaders who came after Manomekh were weak, and their power was divided by warring factions within the nobility. By 1169, Kyiv was seized and looted by one of its own, Prince Andrei Bogolyubsky, who declared himself grand prince and made a new city, Volodymyr, his capital.

By then, however, Kyiv was already losing importance as a trading center. The Crusades, a series of religious wars to regain the Holy Land in the Near East, opened up new trade routes across the Mediterranean, making the route through Kyiv obsolete. The unity of Rus fell apart, and many princes and nobles went their own way. Some moved to the northeast, where in a wilderness they would establish the city of Moscow and develop a new city-state called Muscovy.

Under the Mongols and Poles

Meanwhile in the East, another invading group, led by the great Genghis Khan (1162–1227), was moving west. The Mongols, fearless warriors on horseback, were the greatest conquerors to emerge from Asia. After a series of bloody conflicts, the Mongols conquered Kyiv in 1223. In victory, these fierce intruders showed no mercy. They forced the princes of Kyiv to lie on the ground and then built a wooden platform above them. When the Mongols entered the platform for a feast, the princes were literally crushed to death. Within a decade, nearly all of Kyivan Rus was under Mongol control and would remain so for two centuries.

The Mongol Empire, however, was too far-flung to control, and the Mongols were poor administrators. When their empire began to crumble, the power vacuum they left was quickly filled by Lithuania and then a rising kingdom to the west—Poland. The Poles took over the fallen Kyivan lands, now called Ukrainia, or "borderlands," in 1569. Although bound to the Ukrainians by ethnic background, the Poles did not deal kindly with their conquered neighbors. They seized peasants' land and created a serf system, whereby Ukrainian peasants were treated as little better than slaves, tied for life to the land they worked. Worse still, the Poles imposed their religion, Roman Catholicism, on the devout Orthodox Ukrainians.

Resistance against Polish rule arose among the intelligentsia, which consisted primarily of learned monks living in old established monasteries. They kept the Orthodox faith alive in the books they wrote during these dark times. But there was active resistance, too. Bands of peasant soldiers on horseback rode through the Ukrainian frontier. The Turks called them Kozaks, meaning "outlaws," or "free men," in Turkish.

The Kozaks, or Cossacks in English, were brave and bold warriors and figures of romantic heroism, as this excerpt from an early Ukrainian poem makes clear:

> But my men of Kursk are tried warriors
> Swaddled to the sound of trumpets,
> Lulled beneath helmets,
> Nursed from the point of the spear. . . .
> Their bows are strung, their quivers filled.

Their swords are keen.
Like gray wolves they plunge through the steppe,
Seeking glory for themselves and honor for their
prince.

The Kozaks gained their freedom by fighting for the Poles and the Muscovites against the Tatars, another invader from the east. In return for their military service, the Poles granted the Kozaks many privileges that other Ukrainians did not have. They were free to move about at will and were allowed to govern themselves.

Day of the Kozaks

By the 16th century, the Poles were ready to curtail the Kozaks' powers, which they saw as a threat to their empire. In response, many Kozaks revolted. They became freedom fighters not only for themselves but for all Ukrainians who supported and admired them.

Kozak chieftains were called *hetmen*, and they were democratically elected from within each band or group. One of the most powerful hetmen was Bohdan Khmelnytsky (1595–1657). Khmelnytsky became a Kozak by choice, not birth. He was a member of the gentry and was persecuted by a wealthy Polish family who held a grudge against him. The family burned his home and killed one of his sons. When Khmelnytsky complained to the Polish authorities, they threw him in prison. A friend helped him escape, and he immediately joined the Kozaks. In the spring of 1648, Khmelnytsky led an uprising against the Poles. When the Poles sent a legion of loyal Kozaks to attack Khmelnytsky, they ended up joining his cause.

The Kozaks defeated the Poles in two decisive battles and then marched with thousands of followers to the western border of Poland. Khmelnytsky entered Kyiv in triumph on Christmas Day 1649. But the struggle against Poland would not be won easily. A peace treaty that same year called for a Polish-Ukrainian Commonwealth, but it lasted only a short time before war again erupted.

The Kozaks were now powerful enough to carve out their own independent state within the Ukraine, but they were not strong enough to maintain it without constant struggle with the Poles. In 1654, Hetman Khmelnytsky made a fateful decision that would determine the destiny of his country for centuries to come. He turned to the Russians for help. In exchange for Russia's support in their fight against the Poles, the Ukrainian Kozaks took an oath of allegiance to the Russian czar. The two powers signed the Treaty of Peruyaslav (1654), uniting their countries.

But Russia's motives were more selfish than altruistic. It had its own designs on the rich, fertile Ukraine, which it hoped to take from Poland's grip. Following Khmelnytsky's death in 1657, Russia dropped all pretense of an "alliance." It sent a military force to the Ukraine and appointed a Russian governor to rule it. The Kozaks abruptly shifted their allegiance and joined up with their old enemy Poland to fight the Russians. The combined forces of Kozaks, Poles, and Lithuanians defeated the Russians at the Battle of Konotip in 1659.

It was, however, a temporary victory in a war that the Ukrainians were destined to lose. In 1666, Poland and Russia realigned together and divided the Ukraine between them. Russia took the half that was east of the Dnipro River, and Poland took the half to the west.

Under the Heel of the Russian Empire

Throughout the 18th century, Russian power steadily increased in the Ukraine, while the power of the Kozaks steadily weakened. By 1781, the hetmanate ceased to exist. Around the same time, Poland had fallen to Russia and Austria and was itself partitioned between its neighbors. Western Ukraine, previously under Polish control, now came into Russian hands.

The Russian Empire continued to take the Ukraine's rich agricultural and industrial resources, giving little back. Russian emigrants took over the land, displacing Ukrainian families who had lived there for generations. Some peasants went to work for their new Russian landlords. Although they were allowed to worship freely in their Orthodox churches, new churches could not be built in the Ukrainian style but had to conform to Russian standards.

The Ukrainians seethed inwardly under the czar's rule. They were not alone. Other peoples within the empire, and even inside Russia itself, were unhappy with the czar's autocratic government. Russian aristocrats and other people in many parts of the empire began a secret plot to overthrow the czar. One group of revolutionaries in Kyiv were led by a former army officer Pavel Pestal, who proposed shooting the royal family and then unifying all peoples living within the Russian state.

In December 1825, shortly after the death of Alexander I (1777–1825) and the induction of the new czar, Nicholas I (1796–1855), a group called the Decembrists rose up in St. Petersburg. The czar's loyal troops quickly quelled the revolt in that city, and its leaders were exiled or executed. Nicholas I had been seriously frightened by the attempted revolt. In response, he cracked down on dissent, imposed heavy censorship, and created a secret police force to watch over the population for any signs of discontent. The crackdown made a bad situation worse in Ukraine, but despite the repression, or because of it, by the mid-1800s a national reawakening took place. This movement was led by Ukrainian historian Volodymyr Antonovych (1834–1908) and poet Taras Shevchenko (1814–61), an ex-serf who was also a playwright, painter, and social critic.

In 1905, another revolution broke out in St. Petersburg. This time, Ukraine would be directly involved. A large group of demonstrators led

The Kozak attack on the people of Odesa during the 1905 revolution was brilliantly, if inaccurately, depicted in this unforgettable scene from Sergei Eisenstein's classic silent film Potemkin. (Courtesy The Museum of Modern Art/Film Stills)

by a priest descended on the czar's Winter Palace in St. Petersburg. They were fired on by soldiers in what would come to be called "Bloody Sunday." In the months that followed, assassinations, demonstrations, and other events erupted across the empire.

In the Black Sea, sailors aboard the battleship *Potemkin* mutinied against their officers and sailed their ship to the Ukrainian seaport of Odesa. The people of Odesa welcomed the mutineers as heroes. News of these events reached the czar, and he immediately sent troops to the city. What followed is memorably captured in Russian filmmaker Sergei Eisenstein's classic 1925 film *Potemkin*, as Kozaks attacked the people of Odesa with bayonets drawn. These same Kozaks would at one time have been defending these people instead of killing them.

Revolution and Independence—for a While

The Revolution of 1905 was put down, but the Russian Empire was sick and dying. Nicholas II (1868–1918), successor to Alexander II, was a weak and indecisive leader, surrounded by bad advisers who urged him to keep a firm line with the people. Long-needed reforms were ignored or put off, and when World War I (1914–18) began, the populace felt little patriotic fervor for their country. Thousands of Russian and Ukrainian soldiers died at the front, and the war quickly became an unpopular one.

By March 1917, the Russian people had reached their limit and rebelled. Within weeks, Nicholas stepped down from power, and a provisional government took control of the country. A socialist government led by Alexander Kerensky (1881–1970) proved ineffective, and the Bolsheviks, who were communist revolutionaries, seized power in the October Revolution of 1917. For two years, a bloody civil war was waged between the Bolsheviks and the anticommunists.

In Ukraine, national leaders saw the revolution as an opportunity for independence after 200 years of Russian domination. The Central Council of Ukraine met in Kyiv and declared their land a free republic. On January 22, 1918, the Ukrainian National Republic was born. Professor Mykhaylo Hrushevsky (1866–1934), a scholar and celebrated historian, became its first president.

When World War I ended in November 1918, the Ukrainian National Republic was officially recognized by the Western Allies, including the United States. Even the government of Bolshevik leader V. I. Lenin (1870–1924) recognized the new republic. It looked as though the dream of Ukrainian independence, lost since the days of Kyivan Rus, had at last been fulfilled.

The new national anthem, with words from a 19th-century poem, expressed the people's optimism:

> Ukraine is not yet dead, nor its glory and freedom,
> Luck will smile on us brother—Ukrainians.
> Our enemies will die, as the dew does in the sunshine,
> And we, too, brothers, we'll live happily in our land.

But their happiness would be short-lived. A free Ukraine was an irresistible target to its neighbors. The same civil war that tore much of Russia apart quickly enveloped Ukraine. The Poles, Czechs, and Romanians joined in the fray, hoping to take a chunk of rich Ukraine for themselves. For four years, Ukraine saw little but devastation. The elected government finally fled into exile, and a Communist government, backed by the Red Army, was installed in Kyiv. Western Ukraine, supported by the Poles and Austrians, held out for a time but finally fell to the new Soviet state in March 1921.

Poland signed a treaty with the new Communist government, and once more Ukraine was carved up among the victors, with pieces going to Poland, Romania, and Czechoslovakia. The lion's share of Ukraine, however, was seized by the newly formed Union of Soviet Socialist Republics (USSR). In 1922, Ukraine, along with Belarus, Russia, and Transcaucasia, became one of the first four socialist republics. This federation was controlled by Russia, which allowed the individual republics a certain degree of autonomy. In Ukraine, the Ukrainian language could still be spoken and taught in schools, Ukrainian culture was not suppressed, emigrés who had left during the years of civil war were welcomed back, and the Soviet Union's New Economic Policy (NEP) allowed some privately owned businesses to exist.

It looked as though the future of Ukraine might be far better under the Communists than it had been under the czar. But with Lenin's death in

1924, a new leader came to power. He would unleash such terrors on Ukraine that they would make the years under the czars look idyllic. The real nightmare was about to begin.

NOTES

p. 4 "'We knew not whether . . .'" Robert Wallace, *Rise of Russia* (New York: Time-Life Books, 1967), p. 32.

pp. 7–8 "'But my men of Kursk . . .'" Michael Hrushevsky, *A History of Ukraine* (New Haven, Conn.: Yale University Press, 1941), p. 153.

p. 12 "'Ukraine is not yet dead   '" Linda Hodges and George Chumak, *Language and Travel Guide to Ukraine* (New York: Hippocrene Books, 1994), p. 2.

A SOVIET REPUBLIC (1924 TO 1991)

If Lenin had not died of a stroke in 1924, it is entirely possible he would have tightened the reins on Ukraine and the other Soviet republics. But under the dictatorship of Joseph Stalin (1879–1953) such possibilities became certainties.

In 1928, the year he rose to supreme power in the Soviet Union, Stalin abruptly ended the "honeymoon" with Ukraine, his most valued republic after Russia. He reinstated Russian as the official language and banned the use of Ukrainian. He had thousands of artists, writers, and other intellectuals who were opposed to the Soviet government exiled, imprisoned, or executed. Worst of all, in 1929, he set about to collectivize the 25 million peasant farms in the Soviet Union, a large proportion of which were in Ukraine. Once privately run, these farms would now belong to the state, and in many cases the previous owners would become hired laborers on what once was their land.

Stalin, Khrushchev, and the Great Famine

Nowhere was there more resistance to Stalin's collectivization plan than among the stubborn, independent farmers of Ukraine. Most of them refused to send their valuable grain to Russia or give up ownership of their farms. In some cases, farmers put up armed resistance to the Russian soldiers who came to enforce Stalin's will, fighting them with pitchforks and axes. Millions of peasants and their families were forced to emigrate, while others were arrested and executed. Still others were sent to labor camps, where many of them faced lingering deaths. But the worst fate awaited those left behind on the farms.

To punish the Ukrainians for daring to resist him, Stalin requisitioned every ear of grain and even seeds to be exported to Moscow and other cities to feed urban workers. While the Russian workers ate their bread, the peasants of Ukraine went hungry.

The years 1932 and 1933 saw the worst human-caused famine in recorded history. Stalin caused 7 million Ukrainians—men, women, and children—literally to starve to death. Miron Dolot, who lived through the famine as a child, remembered it vividly:

Death from starvation became daily occurrences. There was always some burial in the village cemetery. One could see strange funeral

The happy faces of these peasant women at a Ukraine collective farm are probably pure Soviet propaganda. Ukrainian farm families stubbornly resisted attempts to make them work on state-run farms. Many paid for it with their lives. (Courtesy Library of Congress)

processions: children pulling homemade hand-wagons with the bodies of their dead parents in them or the parents carting the bodies of their children. There were no coffins; no burial ceremonies performed by priests. The bodies of the starved were just deposited in a large common grave, one upon the other; that was all there was to it. . . .

This horrendous crime, now known as the Great Famine, would make Stalin a much-hated man in Ukraine and contribute to the defection of tens of thousands of Ukrainians a decade later in World War II (1939–45).

In 1938, Stalin appointed one of his protégés, Nikita Khrushchev (1894–1971), as first secretary of the Communist Party in Ukraine. Although Khrushchev was born at Kalinovka on the Ukrainian border, he knew nothing about agriculture, the lifeblood of Ukraine. He tried to decline the appointment, but Stalin knew Khrushchev's ambition and loyalty made him the right man for the job. Kyiv was a hotbed of nationalism when Khrushchev arrived there, and the working-class leadership was dominated by a liberal intelligentsia.

Khrushchev ruthlessly purged the Communist Party of suspect members. By the summer of 1938, only three of the previous 86 members of the Central Committee of the Ukrainian Communist Party were still in office. The hunt for "enemies of the state" grew so hysterical that even Khrushchev himself was shocked by the machinery he had put in motion. In his memoirs, he described the accusation of a man named Medved, a respected Ukrainian doctor and deputy chief of the Regional Health Department:

> . . . some woman got up at a Party meeting, pointed her finger at [Medved], and said, "I don't know that man over there but I can tell from the look in his eyes that he's an enemy of the people." Can you imagine?
>
> Fortunately, Medved didn't lose control of himself. He retorted immediately, "I don't know this woman who's just denounced me, but I can tell from the look in her eyes that she's a prostitute"—only he used a more expressive word. Medved's quick comeback probably saved his life. If he'd let himself be put on the defensive

and had started protesting that he wasn't an enemy of the people, he would have fallen all the more under suspicion, and the woman who denounced him would have been encouraged to press her charge against him, knowing that she wouldn't have to take any responsibility for what happened.

Interestingly, Medved survived these nightmare years and lived to serve in the Ukrainian delegation that helped found the United Nations (UN) in San Francisco in 1945.

The Ravages of War

In September 1939, while secretly in league with the Soviet Union, fascist Nazi Germany, invaded Poland. France and Great Britain were aghast and immediately declared war on Germany. World War II had begun. The Soviet Union remained neutral until Germany broke their treaty and attacked Ukraine and other Soviet territory in June 1941. Many Ukrainians, suffering under Stalin's harsh rule, welcomed the Germans with open arms. German troops marching into Ukrainian villages were showered with flowers and serenaded by peasants dressed in native folk costumes and playing musical instruments. Banners hanging across arches read "The Ukrainian people thank their liberator, the brave German Army. Heil Adolf Hitler!" Some Ukrainians joined the German cause. Even such patriots as Stepan Bandera (1909–59), a leading Ukrainian nationalist, collaborated with the Nazis.

But the Ukrainians had misplaced their hopes. German dictator Adolf Hitler (1889–1945) viewed all Slavs—a diverse group of peoples with a common heritage, living mostly in Eastern Europe—as *Untermenschen*, meaning "subhumans" in German. Hitler believed the Slavs were meant to serve as slaves for his German *Reich* (empire), their natural resources were to be plundered, and their land was to become homes for German immigrants. The invading Germans treated the Ukrainians with as much contempt as Stalin had.

"There is no Ukraine," boasted Nazi leader Erich Koch, who administered the country with ruthless cruelty. When a nationalist damaged a German transmitter in Kyiv, Koch ordered 400 men, chosen at random,

Ukraine was on the front line during the German invasion of the Soviet Union in World War II. Here, Soviet troops attempt to stop the German advance by destroying a bridge over the Styr River. (Courtesy Library of Congress)

to be shot. He also had 38,000 citizens of Kyiv deported to Germany in cattle cars to make room for German settlers.

Realizing their mistake, many Ukrainians turned their allegiance back to the Soviet Union. Others, such as Bandera, formed an underground nationalist army to fight both Germans and Russians.

Ukraine became one of the major battlegrounds on the eastern front, and it was passed back and forth between Germany and Russia like a football. By the war's end in 1945, 6.8 million Ukrainians had died in the fighting or perished from hunger or disease. Several more million had been worked to death in Soviet or German labor and concentration camps. Ukrainian cities, including Kyiv, lay in ruins, and 18,000 villages were completely destroyed. No other European country lost more people in World War II.

Germany's defeat ended the Nazi terror, but the old terror of Stalinism returned as the Soviet Union regained control of Ukraine. Ukrainians returning from German prisons and camps where they had been held prisoner were seen by the paranoiac Stalin as traitors or spies, so they were sent to Soviet labor camps or shot. Execution was the fate for many collaborators, including thousands of Kozaks.

Ukrainian nationalists continued to fight the Soviets with guerrilla tactics. They were led by Bandera, who was now called Taras Bulba, after the Kozak hero of a story by Ukrainian-born Russian writer Nikolai Gogol (1809–52). The nationalists were crushed several years later when the Soviets expended all their efforts against them.

A Second Famine

But even those loyal Ukrainians who did nothing to incur Stalin's wrath were not out of harm's way. A second great famine swept the country in 1946, but this time nature was the villain. The driest summer on record led to a disastrous harvest, with few farmers left to reap what little grain there was.

Khrushchev, now prime minister of the Ukrainian Soviet Socialist Republic, received disturb-ing reports about death from starvation—and even worse. "I read a report that a human head and the sole of feet had been found under a little bridge near Vasilkovo, a town outside of Kyiv," Khrushchev wrote in his

The working people of Kyiv, many of them in traditional folk costumes, commemorate the 300th anniversary of the reunion of Ukraine with Russia in June 1954.
(Courtesy Library of Congress)

autobiography. "Apparently the corpse had been eaten." Despite the high death toll, the Ukrainian famine was kept a secret by the Soviets, and even today little is known about it in the West.

Weak and broken though they may have been, Ukrainians clung steadfastly to an ideal of national unity in the postwar years. The Soviet Union seized western Ukraine from Poland and Czechoslovakia. For the first time in centuries, Ukraine was whole, though enslaved.

Following Stalin's death in 1953, there was a scramble for power in the Soviet Union. Khrushchev emerged the victor by 1956. He denounced Stalin for his crimes against the Soviet people, while conveniently overlooking his own participation in some of those crimes. Ukraine, which Khrushchev knew well from his years as a party leader there, played a central role in his efforts to renew the economy and increase industrial growth. Khrushchev may have been more tolerant than Stalin of Ukrainian culture, but he did not approve of Ukrainian nationalism at Soviet expense, and the Russianization of Ukraine continued. It met strong resistance from a small but resilient dissident movement.

The Rise of Brezhnev

Ukraine's importance to the Soviet Union was not just economic; it was political as well. It produced the next major figure in Soviet politics. Leonid Brezhnev (see boxed biography) hailed from Dneprodzerzhinsk (then called Kamenske) and worked his way up the Communist Party ladder in Ukraine, becoming a major general on the Ukrainian front during World War II.

Brezhnev was one of Khrushchev's protégés, and the Soviet leader helped him advance through the ranks. Shortly before Stalin's death, Brezhnev was appointed to the party's Central Committee in Moscow. In October 1964, Khrushchev fell from power, mainly because government leaders disapproved of his economic policies and his antagonistic stand toward Communist China. Brezhnev helped engineer his mentor's fall and within a short time replaced him as Soviet leader.

Brezhnev made Ukraine virtually a "junior partner" with Russia in the governing of the Soviet Union, but his influence was not all positive. He had little tolerance for any dissent in either the Eastern Europe

LEONID BREZHNEV (1906–1982)

He called himself a "fifth generation steelman," and he could be as resilient as steel when representing the interests of the Soviet Union. But Leonid Brezhnev could also bend to accommodate the world when it suited his purpose.

Brezhnev was born in a working-class neighborhood of Kamenske, a typical industrial Ukrainian town. His father worked in a steel plant, and he himself worked as a stoker, oiler, and fitter while studying at a local metallurgical institute. Brezhnev became a member of the Communist Party in 1931 and steadily worked his way up the political ladder, achieving the rank of major general in the Red Army during World War II.

After the war, he began working closely with Nikita Khrushchev in Ukraine, becoming his protégé. At the 19th Party Congress in 1952, Brezhnev became a full member of the powerful Central Committee. The death of Stalin, another "man of steel," the following year set back Brezhnev's career temporarily, but as Khrushchev rose to power, he brought Brezhnev along with him. Brezhnev administered Khrushchev's program of cultivating "virgin lands" in Central Asia and Siberia to improve agricultural productivity.

In 1964, Brezhnev joined other Soviet leaders in forcing Khrushchev into retirement. Although it was partly Khrushchev's "cult of personality" that had led to his removal, Brezhnev later seized power for himself at the expense of his political partner, Alexei Kosygin.

The leader of the USSR for 18 years, Brezhnev was alternately a stern and an indulgent father to Ukraine and the other Soviet republics. He pursued and achieved a détente (relaxing of tensions) with the United States in the early 1970s, but at the same time, he kept a firm grip on Eastern Europe, invading Czechoslovakia in 1968. He signed numerous nuclear nonproliferation treaties with the United States but encouraged and supported revolutionary movements in developing nations. In December 1979, he sent Soviet troops into Afghanistan to aid the Communist government, which was fighting anticommunist rebels. Afghanistan became the Soviet Union's Vietnam, a disastrous war that dragged on for years after Brezhnev's death.

An adept politician and a skilled negotiator, Brezhnev brought order and security to his country, but he did little to improve the lives of its people. The massive and corrupt bureaucracy he helped perpetuate eventually brought down the Soviet Union and everything he stood for.

Soviet leader Leonid Brezhnev, shown here (left) with Khrushchev, was Ukrainian by birth. The corruption of his last years of power was an unfortunate model for many present-day Ukrainian politicians. (Courtesy Library of Congress)

satellites of the Communist bloc or within the USSR itself. In 1968, he made the decision to invade Czechoslovakia when its government became too liberal. According to what was called "Brezhnev's doctrine," the Soviet Union had the right, even the duty, to intervene domestically in any Communist bloc nation that veered from the strict party line.

As he grew older, Brezhnev relied more and more on his political cronies, many of them from Ukraine, to run the country. Corruption, bribery, and kickbacks became business as usual in the Soviet Union in the 1970s and early 1980s. Government mismanagement wreaked havoc on the once-sturdy Ukrainian economy. This legacy of political corruption would continue to plague the republic of Ukraine long after the collapse of communism.

In November 1982, the 76-year-old Brezhnev died at home of a heart attack. He was replaced in succession by two more old guard communists—Yuri Andropov (1914–84) and Konstantin Chernenko (1911–85) —both of whom were in poor health and died shortly after taking office. In 1985, the Politburo, the governing body of the Soviet Union, chose a younger man as their next leader, one who had new ideas of how to run the Soviet Union.

Mikhail Gorbachev (b. 1931) promised his people "a thorough renewal of every aspect of Soviet life—economic, social, political and moral." To bring about this renewal he instituted a policy of perestroika, which means "restructuring" in Russian, that would change and renew old institutions. He also announced a policy of glasnost, a "loosening of censorship and government restrictions" in social and cultural life.

Gorbachev's liberal policies gave new hope to the Ukrainian nationalists who had been opposed to Soviet domination for decades. But amid hope, a fresh disaster struck Ukraine.

Chornobyl

On April 26, 1986, an explosion ripped off the top of a nuclear power plant at Chornobyl (spelled Chernobyl in the West), in Ukraine, 80 miles (129 km) north of Kyiv. The resulting fires took 31 lives. Another 100,000 people were exposed to high levels of radiation from 11 tons (10 metric tons) of radioactive particles shot into the air.

In a fatal blunder, the Soviet government waited almost two full days before informing the public of the explosion, the worst civilian nuclear disaster to date. Gorbachev, seeking to distance himself from the tragedy, stayed out of the public eye for almost three weeks. The government dismissed nuclear power officials for negligence and published a detailed report on the disaster and its causes. It also passed strict laws to improve safety in nuclear plants. But the damage had been done.

In the months and years following the accident, thousands of people, many of them children, were stricken with cancer, blood diseases, and a host of other illnesses that were a direct result of radiation exposure. For weeks a radioactive cloud stretched out from the Soviet Union to Sweden, Poland, Finland, West Germany, and possibly, some experts believe, the entire Northern Hemisphere, poisoning the environment.

The Ukrainians, who suffered most directly from the accident, rose up in anger to protest the presence of nuclear power plants in their republic. The protest was so vigorous that it forced the government to act. Several Soviet reactors, recently completed, were never opened, while others, still being planned, were abandoned.

The Birth of Rukh

Just as Communist governments in Eastern Europe were being besieged by reformers calling for change, people within the Soviet republics were crying for independence, too. Nowhere was the cry for reform louder than in Ukraine. In September 1989, a popular new movement was born. It called itself Rukh, meaning "movement" in Ukrainian, and it quickly became the voice of perestroika in the republic. Rukh not only spoke up for political change within Ukraine but sought a full accounting of the dark past and Stalin's crimes against the Ukrainian people, especially the Great Famine of 1932–33. In November 1989, Ukrainian Communist Party head Volodymyr Shcherbytskyi was replaced with the more moderate Volodymyr Ivashko. The following March, open elections took place in Ukraine for the first time in nearly 70 years. Members of Rukh and other anticommunist candidates competed with Communists. The alliance of anticommunist groups won a fourth of the seats in the parliament, a significant victory.

To dramatize their cause and commemorate the unification of Ukraine in 1919, Rukh organized half a million Ukrainian men, women, and children into a human chain along the highway linking Kyiv and Lviv. Realizing his reforms were threatening to tear apart the Soviet Union, Gorbachev proposed a treaty to Ukraine and to the other republics. The treaty would give them some autonomy while reserving other powers for the central government. The Ukrainian government was seriously considering signing this union treaty in the summer of 1991 when startling events took place that shook the foundations of the communist system and made a final break with the Soviet Union inevitable.

NOTES

pp. 16–17 "'Death from starvation became . . .'" Miron Dolot, *Sources of the Western Tradition* (Boston: Houghton Mifflin, 2003), p. 343.

pp. 17–18 "'. . . some woman got up . . .'" Nikita Khrushchev, *Khrushchev Remembers* (Boston: Little, Brown, 1970), pp. 114–115.

p. 18 "'The Ukrainian people thank their liberator . . .'" Nicholas Bethell, *Russia Besieged* (Alexandria, Va.: Time-Life Books, 1977), p. 78.

p. 18 "'There is no Ukraine.'" Bethell, p. 83.

pp. 20–21 "'I read a report . . .'" Khrushchev, p. 234.

THE PRICE OF FREEDOM
(1991 TO THE PRESENT)

On Monday, August 19, 1991, the Soviet news media made a stunning announcement: "for health reasons," Mikhail Gorbachev was stepping down from power and passing the reins of government to an eight-man state committee. In truth, Gorbachev and his family were under house arrest at his Black Sea vacation home. Among the eight conspirators in this coup were antireformers within Gorbachev's government: his vice president, prime minister, defense minister, and interior minister. They were bent on ending all reforms and returning the Soviet Union to hard-line communism.

Those who opposed the coup, including newly elected president of Russia Boris Yeltsin (b. 1931), gathered at the parliament building in central Moscow. From atop a tank, Yeltsin delivered a defiant speech and called for a general strike. Yeltsin supporters took to the streets. The resulting demonstrations frightened the coup leaders into using military force, but it was a halfhearted effort. Two people died in street clashes. Within three days the coup fell apart. One of the conspirators committed suicide, and the others were arrested. Gorbachev was released and returned to Moscow.

The failed coup had a galvanizing effect on the impatient republics within the Soviet Union. Not only were the hard-liners shown to be incompetent fools, but Gorbachev himself lost credibility. It was he, after all, who had put the very men who tried to overthrow him in high positions of trust. Here was undeniable proof, many felt, that communism was dying.

Independence Day

On August 24, only days after the coup had ended, the Ukrainian parliament, called the Supreme Council, proclaimed its independence from the Soviet Union. The only authority it would hitherto be accountable to was its own constitution and the laws of the land. The day was declared a national holiday, Ukraine's own independence day. The neighboring republics of Belarus and Moldova, along with Uzbekistan and Kyrgyzstan, were quick to declare their own independence. The Soviet Union, after 70 years of existence, was falling apart.

President Yeltsin, acclaimed by the public for his heroic stand during the coup, was at the height of his popularity and took the bold step of outlawing the Communist Party. The Ukrainian leaders knew they

Ukrainians celebrate their independence from the Soviet Union on August 24, 1991. The date has since become a national holiday. (AP Photo/Efrem Lukatsky)

could take their cause of freedom to the people with no fear of reprisals from Moscow.

In a national referendum held on December 1, 1991, 90 percent of the Ukrainian electorate voted in favor of independence. They simultaneously elected former Communist leader Leonid Kravchuk (b. 1934) as their first president. A week later, Ukraine signed the Minsk Agreement with Russia and Belarus. This agreement had a two-fold purpose. It effectively dissolved the Soviet Union as a political entity and joined the three republics in a loose federation called the Commonwealth of Independent States (CIS). In time, eight other former republics would join the CIS, roughly the equivalent of the British Commonwealth, while Georgia, Lithuania, Latvia, and Estonia chose not to join. Ukraine, a leader in the independence movement, saw the CIS as an intermediate step on the way to complete independence from Russia and its neighbors.

A Trust Betrayed

But freedom from communism did not release Ukraine from other problems. For one thing, Kravchuk, and those who supported him, did not see a break with Russia as an end to privilege for former Communists. Nor did his government believe an independent Ukraine had to follow a strict road to democracy as it was practiced in the West. While the Kravchuk government agreed to work with the reformers of Rukh, which had become a national party, they held the reins of power and kept real reform at a minimum. Subsidies to state-owned businesses continued, and private enterprise was not encouraged.

There was one member of Kravchuk's government, however, who believed reform was inevitable and necessary: Prime Minister Leonid Kuchma (see boxed biography on pages 32/33). Kuchma, who was appointed in 1992, backed economic reform and tried to move forward the process of privatization of state companies and industry. One writer called him the "blunt-spoken new prime minister who told white-elephant industries the free ride was over."

It was a message that made him many enemies among the conservative majority in the Supreme Council, the body he oversaw as prime minister. Council members did everything they could to block his reform

Leonid Kravchuk (right), first president of an independent Ukraine, shares a handclasp with U.S. president Bill Clinton (left) and Russian president Boris Yeltsin in January 1994. In elections only six months later Kravchuk was defeated by his former prime minister, Leonid Kuchma. (AP Photo/Denis Paquin)

bills. Frustrated and disenchanted, Kuchma resigned from office in September 1993, leaving Kravchuk to assume many of the powers of the prime minister.

The Ukrainian people, however, were incensed by Kuchma's resignation and blamed it on the government. A general strike was called. The economy, never very healthy since the fall of communism, plunged into chaos. Under pressure from the public, President Kravchuk was forced to move parliamentary elections from early 1995 to March 1994.

The Election of 1994

The process of democratic elections in Ukraine was one of the longest and most torturous in postcommunist Eastern Europe. The new republic had produced a series of complicated election laws that, among other things, required half the electorate to participate. They also required that a candidate receive more than half the vote to win. It took nearly five months of runoffs and vote counting to elect 360 of the 450 representatives to the Supreme Council.

The final outcome was surprising. The Communists kept their lead in the parliament with 91 seats, Rukh took 30 seats, and 20 were divided among the remaining political parties. But the largest group of elected representatives—219—were aligned with no political party.

Because the parliamentary elections took so long, Kravchuk postponed the presidential election to June 26. His chief rival was Kuchma. In two rounds of voting, Kravchuk was defeated by his former prime minister, who received 52 percent of the vote compared to Kravchuk's 45 percent.

President Kuchma set out in the fall of 1994 to achieve several daunting goals: move economic reform forward, end corruption in the government, and make Ukraine new friends abroad. He gave a speech outlining a new economic program in which he vowed to freeze prices, hasten privatization of land and property, and institute a new stable currency, the *hryunya*. He also found time to visit Canada and the United States that fall.

The visits abroad were meant to strengthen ties with the West and, more important, gain much needed foreign aid and expertise. Following Kuchma's visit, the United States pledged $900 million for the privatization process, making Ukraine the third largest recipient of U.S. foreign aid. Canada gave the new nation more than $17 million in technical expertise. The International Monetary Fund (IMF) pledged $2 billion in loans over a three-year period, but only if Ukraine made a sincere and concerted effort toward market reform.

Corruption Widens

Although he had defeated Kravchuk, Kuchma was saddled with the previous president's cabinet ministers and other government workers. Not until March 1995 was he able to overcome resistance in the Supreme Council and appoint his own advisers.

Although Kuchma himself was personally untainted by corruption, his election drew many corrupt politicians to his administration. Former acting prime minister Yukhim Zvyakilsky was arrested on charges of

LEONID KUCHMA (b. 1938)

Most Ukrainian politicians spend their lives working their way up the party ladder to achieve power. Leonid Kuchma took a very different road to the top, which he achieved with breathtaking swiftness.

He was born in a small village in Ukraine's Chernigiv region. His parents were peasants; his father died during World War II. In 1960, Kuchma graduated from Dnepropetrovsk State University with a degree in mechanical engineering. He soon got a job at Yuzhmash, the largest satellite and rocket factory complex in the world. He would remain there for the next three decades, eventually becoming the company's director in 1986. The company

Leonid Kuchma came to government service relatively late in life. For many years he was an executive with a missile factory. (Courtesy NATO)

embezzlement, and his successor Yevgen Marchchuk (b. 1941) was later fired for self-promotion. In May 1996, Kuchma appointed Pavlo Lazarenko (b. 1953) as the fifth prime minister since independence.

Lazarenko proved to be little better than his predecessors; he soon began appointing officials from his home region of Dnepropetrovsk, where Brezhnev promoted many of his political cronies back in the 1970s. When questioned about this blatant favoritism, Lazarenko replied, "I need my own people."

Even more discouraging, the prime minister helped United Energy Systems, a utility company to which he had close ties, gain a gas had its own Communist Party committee, and Kuchma served as its secretary from 1975 to 1982. His political career, however, did not begin in earnest until 1990, when he was elected to the Ukrainian parliament as a representative from Dnepropetrovsk. He was such an outstanding supporter of economic reform in the newly independent republic that two years later he was appointed prime minister by Ukrainian president Leonid Kravchuk.

Kuchma's program to restructure the economy and throw out corrupt officials quickly earned him the title the "iron minister." But Kuchma could not bend the equally iron will of the legislature. In September 1993, he resigned in frustration. "I am convinced," he said, "Ukraine needs urgent political reforms, without which no economic reforms can occur, and we could well lose our independence."

It was the first notice of a new political campaign, this time for president, which he won handily a year later. Kuchma's program for economic recovery included privatizing three-fourths of all state-owned property by 1997, cutting fat subsidies to state-owned businesses, and lifting of price controls.

Whatever goals Kuchma set for himself were eventually undermined by a powerful regime that brooked no criticism and became increasingly corrupt. Although he won a second term as president, in 1999, Kuchma's reputation became more and more tarnished. The former crusading prime minister has sadly ended up as corrupt as the men he once opposed in government. He will be fortunate if, at the end of his presidency, he is not prosecuted on charges ranging from bribery to coconspiracy to commit murder.

---

distribution monopoly in the region. A controversial figure, Lazarenko was the target of an assassination attempt in July 1996, when a bomb nearly blew up his car as he was riding to the airport.

Kuchma removed Lazarenko from office in 1997. In December 1998, Lazarenko was arrested by authorities in Switzerland for laundering millions of dollars through Swiss bank accounts. Released on bail, Lazarenko fled to the United States, where he was detained by American customs officials for charges against him of embezzlement and misuse of government funds in his homeland. He later moved to California, where he was arrested on charges of money laundering and mail fraud.

After a long investigation, he was convicted of these charges in June 2004. The Ukranian government is continuing efforts to extradite Lazarenko.

Back in the Ukraine, charges of abuse of power were being leveled against Kuchma, too. "People are being hired for their loyalty to political factions rather than their commitment to the reform process," said Slavko Pikhovshesk, director of the Ukrainian Center for Independent Political Research in Kyiv.

Trouble in Crimea

Another domestic problem for the Ukrainian president lay to the south. The Crimea, a peninsula of land jutting into the Black Sea, had been given to Ukraine back in 1954 as a goodwill gesture by Khrushchev. Never in his wildest dreams did Khrushchev think that Ukraine would ever cease to be a part of the Soviet Union and possess the Crimea for itself. The same might be said of many ethnic Russians living in Crimea, who continue to see themselves as Russians first.

When Ukraine became independent in 1991, Crimea's parliament voted to make it an autonomous republic. The Ukrainian republic accepted this but did not accept Crimea's vote for independence from Ukraine in May 1992. The Crimeans persisted. In a runoff presidential election in January 1994, Yuri Meshkov, a Russian nationalist who favored separatism, was elected. To further weaken its ties with Ukraine, the Crimean parliament voted to restore the suspended constitution of 1992, which authorized Crimea's sovereignty as an independent power.

In August 1994, the Crimean city of Sevastopol declared itself a Russian city. Ukraine intervened in March 1995, and a potential rebellion was averted. Over the next two months, Kuchma and the Ukrainian parliament worked tirelessly to bring Crimea back into Ukraine's sphere of influence. They voted to reduce President Meshkov's powers and appointed Anatoley Franchuk, Kyiv's man, as the new prime minister. Meshkov was ousted from power later that same year. In December 1998, the Ukrainian parliament approved a new constitution for Crimea that gave it more autonomy. However, the poor treatment of Crimea's Tatar population has continued the tension in Ukraine's relations with its wayward state.

Russian Relations

For all the troubles facing his country, Kuchma made significant improvements in his first three years as president. By late 1996, most of the economy had been privatized, compared with only 5 percent when Kravchuk left office in 1994. The average monthly wage had risen in that time from $11 to $80. New treaties with Russia lessened tensions between the two countries.

In May 1997, Russian president Boris Yeltsin made his first trip to Ukraine. Meeting with Kuchma, Yeltsin signed a friendship treaty with Ukraine. Standing at the Tomb of the Unknown Soldier, Yeltsin claimed that Russia's relationship with Ukraine "is a priority of priorities for us. We respect and honor the territorial integrity of Ukraine."

But if tensions with Russia relaxed, they did not disappear. Ukraine was still bent on going its own, independent way.

On August 25, 1997, Ukraine celebrated with military exercises the sixth anniversary of its independence from Moscow. Top naval officer Rear Admiral Mikhaylo Yezhel boldly announced that among those participating in peacekeeping exercises at Donuzlav, the Crimean naval base, would be more than 100 American sailors and marines. Never before had such a U.S. military presence been allowed at the base. It was all part of the North Atlantic Treaty Organization's (NATO) Partnership for Peace, which Ukraine joined in 1994.

Kuchma's Second Term

As his first term as president was drawing to a close, Kuchma was in serious trouble. Not only had he failed to root out corruption in his government, but the economy was once again faltering. Going into the election of 1999, Kuchma looked vulnerable. In the grinding round of electoral elimination, one opponent emerged from the field, Communist candidate Petro Simonenko. Despite the failures of his administration, Kuchma managed to raise Ukrainian fears of a return to communism under Simonenko and beat his opponent in the final election, held October 31.

President Kuchma, however, began his second term under a cloud of suspicion. During the campaign, the press had accused him of unfairly manipulating the news media against his opponents and illegally using government funds to pay campaign expenses. Among the administration's most vocal critics was journalist Georgy Gongadze. In September 2000, Gongadze disappeared; six weeks later his headless body was found. Rumors quickly spread that Kuchma was implicated in Gongadze's death, although he denied the charge. In secret recordings of his phone conversations, Kuchma supposedly talked to aides about abducting Gongadze. In December, a large demonstration was held in Kyiv denouncing Kuchma. In June 2004, a convicted murderer in prison for other killings confessed to Gongadze's murder. It is not yet known if he acted alone.

A Tarnished Presidency

The United States, which had been one of Ukraine's greatest benefactors, was troubled by the accusations against Kuchma's government. But nothing prepared them for the charge that in mid-2000 the Ukrainian government had, with the president's knowledge, sold sophisticated radar systems to the dictatorship of Saddam Hussein, the United States's sworn enemy in Iraq. Although Kuchma denied the charge, he would not disclose the records that would prove whether the sale took place or not. U.S. and British investigators arrived in Ukraine in November 2002 to look for evidence of the sale to Iraq, but the information they collected was inconclusive.

The dark shadows that now hung over Kuchma's administration made him a pariah in the West. In 1999, he had been the gracious host at a meeting in Yalta of 14 Baltic and Black Sea nations. Three years later, when he showed up uninvited at a NATO summit meeting in Prague, Czech Republic, he was given a cool reception and seated apart from the U.S. and British representatives.

As his second term wound down, President Kuchma was a man fighting for his political life. In November 2002, he dismissed key members of his government, including reform-minded prime minister Viktor Yushchenko (see boxed biography, chapter 4), whom many see as a serious contender for president in 2004. A week later, Kuchma nominated an old friend, Viktor Yanukovich (b. 1950), governor of Donetsk, as the new prime minister. He was later approved by Parliament. The new

Prime Minister Viktor Yanukovich was handpicked by President Kuchma, who sees him as his possible successor in the presidency. (Courtesy NATO)

constitution, passed in June 1996, limits a president to serving only two terms. However, in December 2003, the Constitutional Court ruled that Kuchma, because he was first elected two years before the constitution was approved, could run for a third term. Given his low ratings with the public, it is unlikely that Kuchma will do so. He may have appointed Yanukovich as prime minister in an attempt to help him become his successor. On the other hand, if Yushchenko or another reformer should win the presidency in 2004, Kuchma might very well have criminal charges brought up against him.

A New Beginning

Recently, Kuchma has made a serious attempt to improve his standing with the United States. In spring 2003, he sent a military battalion to Kuwait to aid the United States in its war against Iraq's Saddam Hussein. After the United States declared major hostilities at an end, Kuchma sent 1,800 Ukrainian peacekeepers to assist the Americans in occupied Iraq in September 2003.

Myroslava Gongadze, the widow of Georgy Gongadze, who now lives in the United States, is pleased to see improved relations with her homeland but is cautious in her praise, commenting, "It would be a mistake to say that this means America has forgiven all of Kuchma's sins. I doubt if

[President] George W. Bush will ever shake Kuchma's hand." Perhaps the U.S. president, along with the people of Ukraine, is waiting to see who will govern Ukraine after Kuchma. In that lies the hope of a better future.

NOTES

p. 29 "'blunt-spoken new prime minister . . .'" Edwards, "Ukraine: Running on Empty," *National Geographic,* March 1993, p. 42.

p. 32 "'I need my own people.'" *Washington Post,* October 27, 1996, CD NewsBank.

p. 33 "'I am convinced Ukraine needs . . .'" 1997 *Current Biography Yearbook* (New York: H. W. Wilson, 1997), p. 283.

p. 34 "'People are being hired for their loyalty . . .'" *Washington Post,* October 27, 1996, CD NewsBank.

p. 35 "'is a priority of priorities . . .'" *New York Times,* June 1, 1997, p. 13.

p. 37 "'It would be a mistake . . .'" *Los Angeles Times,* July 5, 2003, p. A3.

PART II
Ukraine Today

4

GOVERNMENT

Since its independence in 1991, Ukraine has been a nation politically at odds with itself. While it has had its differences with Russia and the United States, its internal conflicts have been perhaps even more damaging to its future. Similar to other new nations in Eastern Europe that were long dominated by communism, Ukraine has had to face the double challenge of creating a new market economy while at the same time forging a democratic government that is responsive to the needs of its people.

A Powerful President

Despite its similarities to other Eastern European countries, the government of postcommunist Ukraine is unique in some important ways. Most of its neighbors have followed the English model of a parliamentary system in which the prime minister is the chief executive. In Ukraine, as in the United States, the president is the chief executive. The Ukrainian president is the person who signs legislation into law. He is also the commander in chief of the armed forces.

The prime minister is head of the president's Council of Ministers, which aids and oversees the president's duties. Members of the council are nominated by the president and are confirmed by the Ukrainian parliament, called the Verkhovna Rada, or Supreme Council.

President Kuchma, who has been in office since June 1994, increased the presidential powers dramatically a year after entering office by pushing a "constitutional treaty" through the Supreme Council. It gave the president powers to appoint and dismiss without parliament's approval and gave him the right to rule by decree when he felt necessary, such as in a national emergency. A year later, these measures were incorporated into a new national constitution, which many people felt was long overdue. (Ukraine was one of the few former Soviet republics that did not draft a new constitution after gaining independence.)

The new constitution also allowed Ukrainians to own private property, abolished local councils that were against reform, and made Ukrainian the country's official language. The Supreme Council approved the document after an exhaustive 23-hour session on June 28, 1996.

The constitutional changes were not simply the work of a power-mad leader. When he came into office, the Supreme Council blocked Kuchma's every effort to reform the economy and liberalize the government. He was not even able to appoint his own people in government during his first six months in office but had to contend with those appointments made by his predecessor, Leonid Kravchuk.

The Supreme Council and the Supreme Court

The power of the Ukrainian legislature is nearly equal to that of the president. Unlike a number of other Eastern European countries, the Ukrainian parliament consists of one, not two, houses. The 450 deputies of the Supreme Council enact laws, approve the national budget, and declare war with the president's approval. Deputies serve four-year terms. Half, or 225, of the seats in the Supreme Council are distributed proportionally among the political parties that gained at least 4 percent of the last national electoral vote. The other half are elected by popular vote.

The current council is dominated by Our Ukraine, a coalition of center-right political parties led by former prime minister Viktor Yushchenko (see boxed biography), which controls 25 percent of the seats. The Communist Party, led by Petro Simonenko, has 15 percent of the seats, and

VIKTOR YUSHCHENKO (b. 1954)

The leader of the opposition to the Kuchma government, Viktor Yushchenko is seen by many Ukrainians as the best and brightest hope for their country's future.

He was born in the village of Horuzhivka and attended Ternopil Academy of National Economy, where he earned a degree in accounting and economics. Yushchenko became branch director of the Soviet State Bank in Ulyanivsk in 1976 and over the next decade steadily worked his way up to governor of the postindependent National Bank of Ukraine.

A leading economic reformer whose American wife once worked at the White House as a national security aide, Yushchenko is popular both at home and in the United States. He was appointed prime minister by President Kuchma in December 1999 and dismissed three years later. Since then, Yushchenko has become the leader of the Our Ukraine coalition of moderates and poses the biggest threat to Kuchma's followers in the 2004 presidential election. In February 2003, Yushchenko visited the United States and received a warm reception from President Bush. "Yushchenko is the only hope for Ukraine," said Anders Asland of the Carnegie Endowment for International Peace.The results of one Ukrainian poll showed that if the election for president had been held in 2003, Yushchenko would have won over the other six declared candidates. However, the

(continues)

Former prime minister and head opposition leader Viktor Yushchenko makes a point during a press conference in Kyiv in March 2002.
(AP Photo/Victor Pobedinsky)

(continued)

government's control over the media could prevent him from winning the presidency in 2004, something Yushchenko readily admits. "We need to work together to make sure that elections in Ukraine are fair and democratic," Yushchenko has said. "It's the only thing that democratic forces in Ukraine really need."

the pro-Kuchma For a United Ukraine coalition has somewhere between 7 and 15 percent.

The judicial branch of government is headed by the Supreme Court, which consists of five judges who are elected by the Supreme Council to terms of five years. Again, this court differs significantly from others in the Western world. Constitutional issues, usually the domain of supreme courts, are handled by the Presidium of the Supreme Council, a smaller group within the council. The Presidium is made up of 19 members, including a chairperson and two vice presidents.

The Ukrainian Supreme Court deals with criminal and civil cases of national importance. "People's courts," elected by the voters, hear local judicial cases.

Local Government

Ukraine is divided into 24 provinces, or oblasts, and one autonomous republic, Crimea. Each oblast is named for its capital city and is further divided into counties, or *rayons*. A legislative council and an executive officer elected directly by voters run each oblast and rayon.

National Security

Ukraine's armed forces consist of less than half a million soldiers, not including the Black Sea naval fleet. The big question for Russia and Ukraine's friends in the West has been its nuclear weapons cache.

Ukraine was a Soviet stronghold for nuclear weapons prior to independence. Both Russia and the West were nervous about what an independent Ukraine might do with these weapons.

In December 1991, the nuclear weapons were placed under collective CIS control. This control was abolished in 1993, at which time the Ukrainian government laid claim to all nuclear weapons in its territory.

It was not until November 1994 that Ukraine signed the Nuclear Non-Proliferation Treaty, agreeing to transfer all nuclear weapons to Russia to be dismantled over a seven-year period. In return, Russia agreed to cancel much of Ukraine's debt. Both the United States and Russia guaranteed Ukraine's future nuclear security.

On June 1, 1996, at a ceremony in south Ukraine, the last nuclear warheads were transferred to Russia. In a symbolic gesture, three defense ministers from Ukraine, the United States, and Russia, planted sunflowers on the site of a former Soviet missile silo.

It has taken longer to settle the issue of the Black Sea fleet. The Russians felt the fleet was theirs, while Ukraine countered that it was on Ukrainian soil and thereby at least partly its possession. After years of frustrated negotiations, the two nations finally reached an agreement in June 1995: Russia would get 82 percent of the fleet, and Ukraine, 18 percent. Ukraine also gave Russia control of the fleet base at Sevastopol in exchange for Russian energy supplies and a further reduction of its debt.

Ukraine's position between Russia and the West still makes it feel vulnerable to an outside attack. Its future security may be decided by its efforts to become a full member of NATO, joining such countries as Poland, Hungary, and the Czech Republic, who became NATO members in 1999.

A member of NATO's Partnership for Peace program since 1994, Ukraine began the application process for full membership in May 2002. "There is no future for Ukraine if it remains outside the [NATO] bloc," said Security Minister Yevgeny Marchuk.

The Kuchma government has tried to repair its tarnished international image by supporting NATO efforts. In 1999, Ukraine sent peacekeeping troops to the NATO coalition in Kosovo, the war-torn republic of the former Yugoslavia. In 2003, it was one of 24 countries that sent reinforcement troops to U.S.-occupied Iraq.

While these actions have improved Ukraine's reputation, there are still problems facing the Ukrainian armed forces. Mired in a stagnant economy, the nation cannot afford to bring the military system up to NATO standards, yet the dilemma of faulty equipment and poor leadership was dramatically and tragically demonstrated at an air show in the city of Lviv in July 2002. A fighter jet crashed into a crowd of spectators while performing an acrobatic stunt. Some 85 people were killed and 116 injured. It was one of the worst air show disasters in history and led President Kuchma to fire air force commander Volodymyr Stulnykov. If Ukraine is to be formally invited to join NATO in 2006, with accession two years later, it will largely depend on what progress it can make in both military and domestic issues in the interim.

Foreign Relations

Ukraine's tentative situation with NATO and its problems with the United States have made for closer relations with Russia. Russian president Vladimir Putin (b. 1952), Yeltsin's successor, has helped Ukraine with financial aid and trade. Today Russia supplies 70 percent of Ukraine's energy and is its largest export partner. "Before, Ukraine was like a buffer zone between Russia and the West," said political writer Volodymyr Polokhalo. "Today, Ukraine is transforming itself into a transit country into Russia. Putin is following a very wise policy that uses the weaknesses in Ukraine to his own strength."

The United States does not seem troubled by the developing relationship between Ukraine and its former cold war opponent. After the fall of communism, the United States looked to Ukraine to be a leader in Eastern Europe's movement to democracy. With that hope gone, it sees Ukraine, if able to help itself, as a stable influence on Russia. "A stable, confident and reforming Ukraine would be the kind of neighbor that could encourage a reform-minded Russia on its own transition path," observed U.S. ambassador to Ukraine Carlos Pascual.

Although Western Europe has been cool toward the Kuchma government in recent years, Ukraine has forged stronger ties with other former Soviet republics. In January 2003, Kuchma was nominated by the Russians to a leadership role in the CIS. Back in May 1997, Kuchma and Polish prime minister Alexander Kwaśniewski signed a Declaration of Accord and Unity to end hostile relations between their two nations that go back to the 17th century. More recent conflicts are also being put aside, such as the killing of 35,000 Poles by Ukrainian national insurgents during World War II and the forced resettlement of 150,000 Ukrainians within Poland shortly after the war. Closer ties with Poland and other Eastern European neighbors will gain Ukraine the kind of international approval it needs to forward its cause with both Russia and the West.

NOTES

p. 43 "'Yushchenko is the only hope . . .'" News from Ukraine, available online, URL: http://www.unian.net/eng/news/news-33446.html, downloaded April 4, 2003.

p. 44 "'We need to work together . . .'" News from Ukraine, available online.

p. 45 "'There is no future for Ukraine . . .'" New York Times, May 25, 2002, p. A7.

p. 46 "'Before Ukraine was like . . .'" New York Times, January 13, 2002, p. 3.

p. 46 "'A stable, confident and reforming Ukraine . . .'" New York Times, January 13, 2002, p. 3.

5

RELIGION

"Our church is a wonder to all surrounding lands, and so that the like cannot be found in all the northern lands, nor in the east nor the west," wrote Hilarian, the metropolitan, or archbishop, of the Orthodox Church in Kyiv nearly a thousand years ago.

This was no idle boast. During the time of Kyivan Rus's power, the Orthodox Church was a force to be reckoned with in nearly every area of life. It built monasteries, schools, and poorhouses. It was at the center of Slavic culture and nationhood.

The Ukrainian Orthodox Church remains the largest religion in Ukraine, with 35 million followers in 2000. It is a potent symbol of Ukrainian nationalism, even after 70 years of communism.

Perhaps no people in Eastern Europe, outside of the Poles, remain as devoted to their Christian faith as the Ukrainians. Yet, unlike Poland, Ukraine has for centuries had a deep division in its church, brought about, as so many of its problems have been, by the Poles and Russians.

A Church Divided

The Ukrainian Orthodox Church's power was broken during the Mongol invasion and the subsequent domination of western Ukraine by the Lithuanians and the Poles. Yet it remained the repository of Ukrainian national feelings when there was no political nation. While the Mongols discouraged Christianity in any form, the Poles, devout Roman Catholics, tried to force their brand of Christianity onto the Orthodox Ukrainians. Some converted to Catholicism, but many more resisted.

Realizing that the western Ukrainians would not abandon their religion, the Poles struck a compromise. According to the Union of Brest in 1596, those Orthodox Ukrainians who wished could retain the rites and beliefs of their faith if they would recognize the Roman pope as their spiritual leader. These Ukrainians—both lay people and religious—became known as Ukrainian, or Greek, Catholics.

When western Ukraine was taken over by the Russians after the partition of Poland in the late 18th century, the Ukrainian Orthodox Church was absorbed into the larger Russian Orthodox Church. While the practices and tenets of these two national churches was nearly identical, the Russians saw the nationalism of the Ukrainian church as a threat to their power.

After the Russian Revolution, the newly independent Ukraine republic revived the Ukrainian Orthodox Church. When the republic came under the authority of the Communists a few years later, so did their church. The Communists, avowed atheists, outlawed the Orthodox faith and drove it underground. The Ukrainian Catholic Church, on

Agaphangel, a metropolitan (archbishop) of the Ukrainian Orthodox Church, blesses a Ukrainian woman outside Moscow's Christ the Savior Cathedral during the Archbishops' Council in August 2000. (AP Photo/ Mikhail Metzel)

the other hand, continued to flourish in western Ukraine, which was back under Polish control.

Poland fell to the Germans in World War II. In 1946, it was taken over, along with western Ukraine, by the Communists. Ukrainian Catholic priests were accused by the Communists of collaborating with the Nazis, and many priests were imprisoned or executed. The Ukrainian Catholic Church was outlawed, and its members were forced to join the Ukrainian Orthodox Church, which was given some freedom by the Communists. While they did not approve of any church, the Communists felt it would be easier to control one national church than two.

Ukrainian Catholics who continued to worship in their own church did so at great risk. Even children were discouraged from worshipping. Andrew Palamar, a 19-year-old from Lviv who is studying at a Ukrainian Catholic seminary in the United States, recalls having a necklace with a cross pulled off his neck by a physical education instructor at school. The incident only strengthened his faith. "You feel it more," he said. "Someone says to you: 'Don't do this.' It makes you want to do it more."

The Ukrainian Churches Today

As the Communist state crumbled in Ukraine at the end of the 1980s, the Ukrainian Catholic Church reemerged from the underground. Many Ukrainians were surprised to learn that there were 4 to 7 million church members under communism. In 1990, both the Ukrainian Orthodox Church and the Ukrainian Catholic Church were officially reinstated. Ukrainian Catholic churches, such as St. George's Cathedral in Lviv, which had been taken over by the Ukrainian Orthodox Church during the Communist era, were returned to the Catholics.

"Serving here is like being beside a person who has awakened from a nightmarish sleep," said Reverend Kenneth Nowakowski, a Ukrainian-Canadian serving at St. George's. "When I came in 1991, people were lined up outside every day. I thought they wanted me to do something for them, but they only wanted to talk. About how they had suffered—just to be heard for the first time."

In August 1992, the leaders of both Ukrainian churches—Catholic and Orthodox—agreed to sit down in Oxford, England, to discuss their differences. The Kyivan Cell Study Group, made up of bishops, priests, and theologians for both churches, met to pursue a path toward eventual union without cutting ties to either the Roman pope or his Orthodox counterpart in Moscow, the patriarch, both of whom blessed their mission. If the "Church of Kyiv" can again unite, after four centuries of division, it will be a major step forward for the struggling Ukrainian nation.

But there are other challenges facing the Ukrainian Orthodox Church. In 1991, Ukrainian cleric Filaret broke away from the main Orthodox Church, which still owes allegiance to Moscow, to form a purely nationalistic Orthodox Church. He was excommunicated by the Moscow patriarch, Aleksei II. Since then, Patriarch Filaret has sought to unite his splinter church with the larger Ukrainian Autocephalous Orthodox Church, which is also independent of the Ukrainian and Russian Orthodox Churches.

Tensions between Ukrainian and Russian Orthodox followers, 7.5 million of whom live in Ukraine, peaked in September 1996 when then Russian president Boris Yeltsin signed a religious law singling out the Russian Orthodox Church for special privileges in the republics of the former Soviet Union. Shortly after, a cathedral and seminary owned by the Ukrainian Orthodox Church outside Moscow was seized by the Russian Church.

A Papal Visit

In June 2001, John Paul II made his fourth visit to Ukraine since becoming pope. Ostensibly, the visit was to honor the Roman Catholics martyred during the Soviet era, but another motive was to strengthen ties with the Ukrainian Orthodox Church. It is the pope's fervent hope that one day the two churches—Roman Catholic and Orthodox—divided for a thousand years, will be reunited.

"I wish to assure them [Orthodox followers] that I have not come here with the intention of proselytizing," the pope said on his visit. Many Ukrainian and Russian Orthodox clergy and their followers, however, did not believe him. They fear that the reunification the pope seeks will mean the end of their church. Among those who shunned the pope's five-day visit was the metropolitan Vladimir. "We pray for the preservation of our people in the pure Orthodox faith," said one Orthodox priest, "and to prevent the invasion of our Holy Rus." Patriarch Filaret, on the other hand, welcomed the pope's visit and felt no fear of being undermined by it.

The pope was warmly received in western Ukraine by its 5 million Ukrainian Catholics and 500,000 Roman Catholics. Since this papal visit little improvement has been seen in Roman Catholic–Orthodox relations.

Ukrainian Jews

The Jewish population of Ukraine was substantial up until World War II when hundreds of thousands of Ukrainian Jews perished in Nazi concentration camps or at deportment centers. The worst killing occurred outside Kyiv at a ravine called Babi Yar. On September 29, 1941, about 35,000 Ukrainian Jews were marched to the ravine and then shot to death by German Nazis wielding machine guns. The killing took two days. It is one of the bloodiest massacres in recorded history, and regrettably, local Ukrainian police assisted the Germans.

Some Ukrainian Christians tried to save their Jewish neighbors from Hitler's Holocaust. Father Emilian Kovtch (1884–1944), a parish priest, baptized many Jews in his village near Lviv to save them from Nazi persecution. The Nazis arrested him for doing so in December 1942. When he refused to stop trying to save Jews, he was sent to the Maydanek concentration camp in Nazi-occupied Poland where he died in March 1944. Father Kovtch was among the Catholic martyrs honored by Pope John Paul II on his visit to Ukraine in June 2001.

Today only about 500,000 Jews, representing 1 percent of the population of Ukraine, remain and live mostly in the cities of Kyiv, Odesa, Kharkov, Dnepropetrovsk, and Lviv. In the 1970s, the Soviets first allowed Ukrainian Jews to emigrate. Since then, most Jews have moved to Israel and elsewhere.

Despite their low numbers, Ukrainian Jews are a visible minority in the intellectual and cultural life of the country. In 1993, Solomon's University was established in Kyiv, one of only four Jewish universities in the former Soviet Union. The following year a training center for teachers in Jewish schools in Ukraine, Belarus, and Moldova was founded in Kyiv.

UKRAINE'S JEWISH MYSTIC

Although he died more than 180 years ago, Rabbi Nachman of Bratslav (1772–1810) continues to exert a powerful influence in his adopted country. A Jewish mystic who lived and died in the city of Uman, Nachman urged his followers to commune with nature in solitude, a message not unlike that of the Christian Saint Francis.

For a century after his death, Uman was a place of pilgrimage for Nachman's ultra-Orthodox followers, the Bratslav Hasidim. The pilgrimages to his grave in a Jewish cemetery were stopped when the Communists took over. In 1937, they converted the Uman synagogue into a factory.

In 1988, 250 pilgrims were allowed to visit the rabbi's grave site for the first time in more than 70 years. Since then, the number of pilgrims has swelled, peaking at 7,000 in 1996. The goodwill gesture of the Ukrainian government was partly political. The nation saw it as an opportunity to improve its relations with Israel and bring much-needed revenue to Ukraine. A recent incident, however, may cause them to rethink this policy.

In November 1996, two young fanatical followers of Rabbi Nachman attempted to dig a tunnel under the graveyard, steal his corpse, and return it to Jerusalem. They were caught and sent back to Israel. The Ukrainian government does not want to end the pilgrimages to Uman, but it is concerned about security at the old and historic Jewish graveyard where Nachman is buried. This problem is another example of how politics affect religion in this land of many religions.

Other Religious Groups

There are some 200 Roman Catholic parishes in Ukraine with about 500,000 members, mostly Poles and Hungarians living in western Ukraine. There are also about 2 million Protestants. Since communism's fall, several Protestant denominations have made serious inroads in Ukraine. The two biggest are the Ukrainian Baptist Church and the Ukrainian Evangelical Alliance. There are also sizable numbers of Lutherans, Methodists, and Mormons.

These Hasidic Jews are just a handful of the thousands of Rabbi Nachman's followers from 22 countries who have come to Uman in September 1998 to celebrate the start of the Jewish New Year at his grave. (AP Photo/Efrem Lukatsky)

The Crimea is home to Ukraine's 250,000 Muslim population, which is nearly all Tatar. This area was part of the Turkish Ottoman Empire from the 1400s to 1783, when it was annexed by the Russians. Despite periods of persecution and indifference, the Tatar Muslims of the Crimea have remained devoted to their faith and send their children to Islamic schools.

While the Ukrainian Orthodox Church remains the religion of a majority of Ukrainians, as many as 60 different religions have adherents in Ukraine and have the freedom to worship under the new, postindependence constitution. Hopefully this tolerance, in conjunction with strong spiritual values, will help Ukrainians find a moral center that was painfully eroded during seven decades of Communist rule.

NOTES

p. 49 "'Our church is a wonder . . .'" Robert Wallace, *Rise of Russia* (New York: Time-Life Books, 1967), p. 32.

p. 51 "'You feel it more . . .'" *New York Times*, December 1, 1996, Connecticut section, p. 8.

p. 51 "'Serving here is like . . .'" Mike Edwards, "Ukraine: Running on Empty," *National Geographic*, March 1993, p. 52.

pp. 52–53 "'We pray for the preservation . . .'" *New York Times*, June 23, 2001, p. A3.

p. 52 "'I wish to assure them . . .'" *New York Times*, June 24, 2001, p. 8.

6

ECONOMY

Since earliest times, Ukraine has been blessed with fertile soil, a temperate climate, rich natural resources, and a people for whom technology has always held a strong attraction. Outside of Russia, no republic within the Soviet Union contributed so much to the Soviet economy. Yet in the post-Soviet era, despite all these advantages, Ukraine's economy has stumbled and fallen. This chapter will present the reasons for this failure, while looking at the strengths and weaknesses of the Ukrainian economy, both past and present, and what the future holds.

The Soviet Union's Economic Mainstay

It is no exaggeration to say that the Soviet Union could not have survived without the economic wealth of Ukraine. This one republic supplied the Soviets with one-fourth of their industrial product, one-fourth of all their agricultural produce, one-third of all meat, one-half of all iron ore, and one-third of all steel.

All this abundance both helped and hurt Ukraine. On one hand, it gave Ukraine special status among the republics, even, at times, special privileges that others did not enjoy. On the other hand, the system of Soviet central management that distributed all goods was costly and wasteful. Much of the riches from factories and farms were funneled elsewhere in the Soviet Union and neither fed nor profited Ukrainians.

Residents of Kyiv shop for second-hand clothes at a market on the eve of Ukraine's second free parliamentary elections. Like these shoppers, voters rummaged through dozens of political parties to find which could successfully revive the faltering economy. (AP Photo/Efrem Lukatsky)

Amid fields of ripe crops, Ukrainian peasants too often went hungry. Those few who did reap riches were the corrupt Communist officials and politicians, the legacy of the Brezhnev era.

When Ukraine broke with the Soviet Union and announced its independence, it was with the hope that it would establish a free open-market economy, independent of the Soviet system. But the subsequent breakup of the Soviet Union hurt Ukraine nearly as much as it did Russia. The two republics economically depended heavily on each other.

Breadbasket of the Commonwealth

Southern Ukraine is the steppe, a region covered by short grasses that receive only 10 to 20 inches (25 to 50 cm) of rain a year. The steppe has a rich, black soil (*chernozem*) that is perfect for raising crops, especially grains such as wheat, rye, flax, and barley. The grassland is ideal for live-stock grazing. Irrigation of the steppes has led to the growth of fruit trees and vegetables such as tomatoes, peppers, and melons. Ukraine is the world's leading producer of sugar beets that are processed to make sugar.

The grain of the Ukraine had been used to make the bread that fed millions in the Soviet Union. It earned the region the name the Bread-basket of the Soviet Union and more recently, the Breadbasket of the Commonwealth of Independent States.

Northern Ukraine is also important agriculturally. The cooler climate and less fertile soil is excellent for producing potatoes, rye, flax, and sun-flowers. The seeds of the sunflowers are eaten by animals and people or crushed for their rich oil. Dairy cattle are raised in the north and beef cat-tle in the south, where there are more natural pastures for grazing. Other important livestock includes pigs, sheep, goats, and poultry. Bees are raised for their honey and wax.

The state farms and collective farms of the Soviet era still exist and are only being phased out gradually. Agricultural production has been contracted out to smaller private farms, mostly family owned. Since the Gorbachev era, family farmers have been encouraged to expand the operation of gardens, fruit orchards, and livestock. The state farms have administrated the work, but dismantling this elaborate system can only be done at great cost. To date, only about 2 percent of farms are privately owned.

Many young people, such as Ihor Mychajlyshyn, who now lives in Lviv, have left the family farms. "The people who knew how to farm are the old ones," he explained. "People like me might go back, but we don't know how to work the land. Anyway, there's hardly any equipment."

Treasures from the Earth

If the Ukraine soil is rich, what lies under it is just as precious. Few nations in the world have as much mineral wealth. Mining, an industry here for generations, produces vast amounts of coal, iron ore, and man-ganese ore used in manufacturing steel and cast iron. Other valuable minerals include aluminum, titanium, graphite, marble, gemstones, and the most precious of metals, gold. Salt deposits are, in some places, more

A COAL MINER'S LIFE

In the rich coal mines of the Donets Basin near Donetsk, coal mining is a way of life with a long and proud tradition. Before independence, the Donets Basin produced one-third of the coal for the Soviet Union.

Today, coal miners are among the highest paid workers in Ukraine, although their pay has often been deferred due to economic instability.

Miners pass by a coal pit in Ukrainsk in the coal-rich Donetsk region. Coal miners face many hardships in Ukraine today. (AP Photo/Efrem Lukatsky)

than 600 feet (183 m) thick. It is doubtful Ukraine will ever run out of this useful mineral.

Clay is also mined and used in everything from pottery to soap. One kind of pure white clay, called kaolin, is used in high-grade ceramics, medicines, and textiles and as a coating for paper.

Oil is produced in the western foothills of the Carpathian Mountains and refined at Lviv and Drogabych. Natural gas is produced at Dashera and Shebeliska. Both these energy resources are limited. Ukraine has found itself having to import fuel from other countries within the CIS. Uranium deposits have been used to fuel nuclear reactors, but the disaster at Chornobyl has called into question the future of nuclear power as an energy source in the country (see chapter 10).

Industrial Giant

Industry is the lifeblood of Ukraine, although some types, such as military armaments, have suffered since the end of the cold war and the

"The money isn't the only thing," says miner Viktor Anatoly. "My father and grandfather were coal miners. We're a dynasty."

Well paid as they are, these miners work under the most hazardous conditions. Between 1997 and 1999, nearly 900 miners were killed in Ukraine's more than 200 coal mines. In August 2001, an explosion of methane gas killed more than 27 miners in the Zasiadko mine. An estimated 75 percent of Ukraine's coal mines have hazardous levels of flammable methane gas that can be ignited by the slightest spark.

Much of the anthracite coal has been removed in these mines, and extracting what is left can be difficult. Miners often use large cutting wheels to slice off the coal, another job hazard. In addition, there are the occupational diseases, such as bronchitis and black lung, that they can contract.

While proud of their work in providing coal and energy to a struggling nation, Ukraine's coal miners are more and more speaking out and striking for better and safer working conditions. While the government recognizes the urgent need for overhauling the coal industry, progress has been slow.

Soviet Union's collapse. Overall industrial output grew by more than 14 percent in 2001, and 32 percent of all workers are employed in mining or manufacturing.

Among the leading industries are coal, electrical power, machinery and transportation equipment, chemicals, and ferrous and nonferrous metals. The food-processing industry is extensive and includes meat processing and packing plants, dairies, fruit and vegetable canneries, and sugar refineries where sugar is extracted from sugar beets.

Trade

There have been positive signs in trade growth since 2000. The gross domestic product (GDP) showed an export growth of 6 percent, the first such growth since independence. Russia remains Ukraine's leading trading partner in both exports and imports. Top exports include ferrous and nonferrous metals, chemicals, machinery and transportation equipment, fuel and petroleum products, and food products. Other important export partners are Turkey, Italy, Germany, and the United States.

Ukraine's number one import is energy, in the form of natural gas and electricity. Other leading imports are chemicals, machinery, and equipment. Its main import partners, after Russia, are Turkmenistan, Germany, Italy, and Belarus.

Ukraine will not become a member of the European Union (EU), a trading bloc of 15 European nations, any earlier than 2007. However, it may well benefit from the accession in 2004 of 10 other countries, mostly in Eastern Europe. "With the EU's borders coming to Ukraine's frontier, high European labor costs will force production-intensive industries to look to countries such as Ukraine," believes Myron Wasylyk, a senior vice president of a public relations firm.

Tourism

Tourism is one of the fastest growing sectors of the large Ukraine service industry. In 1998, there were about 2 million foreign tourists in Ukraine, 16 times the number who visited the country in 1992, the first full year of independence. The number-one vacation destination is the Crimea, with its beaches and resorts on the Black Sea. Other popular places for tourists include the Carpathian Mountains, with its skiing facilities, and such historic cities as Kyiv, Kharkiv, and Odesa. Ukraine's proximity to other popular tourist countries, such as Russia and Turkey, is an added attraction for multicountry package tours from abroad. In early 2002, a new government program was approved that would allow some foreign visitors to enter the country without visas and halt the common practice of overcharging foreigners for transportation and accommodations.

Banking, Finance, and Foreign Investment

The Ukrainian unit of money, the hryvnia, was first introduced in 1992. The coin has a proud tradition in Ukraine. The original hryvnia, a coin, was issued 1,000 years ago by Valdymyr the Great.

Financially, Ukraine has not been in sound shape since independence. Those Western businesses that were interested in gaining a toehold in Ukraine after independence were quickly disillusioned. Corrupt officials favored Ukrainian businesses over foreign ones and drove out many investors and businesspeople from abroad. Top U.S. companies, such as Motorola, abandoned plans to open businesses in Ukraine.

Those foreign businesses that tried to stick it out and stand up to corruption were threatened with violence, even death. "It's all rooted in one thing," claimed American businessman David Swure in 1996, "total, unequivocal corruption."

Under the Kuchma government, Ukraine has become more receptive to foreign investment and business, but the administration's corruption and repression of democratic rights has also driven away many Western businesses. While Russia has stepped into this vacuum and put money into Ukraine, it is not the kind of investing that will make the economy strong in the long run. "In most cases," said presidential adviser Anatoly Halchynsky, "the Russian capital comes here via shadowy schemes and worsens our problems by expanding the shadow economy." Halcyhynsky and others would like to see more foreign ties to the West, but any great investment of Western resources seems unlikely before the end of Kuchma's presidency.

The Future

Years of stagnation under corrupt governments that continued the communist system of cronyism have left Ukraine in an economic shambles. A decade of potential economic transition and growth was lost, leaving Ukraine trailing behind most of the other countries in the former Soviet bloc. Since 1999, things have been steadily, if modestly, improving. It may be years, however, before there are significant gains for the average Ukrainian. In 2001, some 29 percent of the population was living below the poverty line. The average monthly wage for workers was about $40. While the official unemployment rate was only 3.8 percent in 2000, this figure did not include the millions of underemployed people who barely scrape by. The national external debt in 2002 was $14.2 billion.

President Kuchma's promises at the start of his second term to reduce the great bureaucracy he inherited from the Soviets, encourage business entrepreneurs, and overhaul the convoluted tax system have only been partially fulfilled. Little meaningful progress has been made in the privatization of agriculture and land. While economic growth has been modest, it has been stable and steady for several years. With Kuchma's departure, better and brighter economic days may lie ahead if an open, democratic, and corruption-free administration takes over.

NOTES

p. 59 "'The people who knew how to farm . . .'" Mike Edwards, "Ukraine: Running on Empty," *National Geographic*, March 1993, p. 52.

pp. 60–61 "'The money isn't the only thing . . .'" Mike Edwards, "Ukraine," *National Geographic*, May 1987, p. 617.

p. 62 "'With the EU's borders coming . . .'" *Los Angeles Times*, July 5, 2003, p. A3.

p. 63 "'It's all rooted in one thing . . .'" *New York Times*, April 9, 1997, p. A3.

p. 63 "'In most cases . . .'" *Los Angeles Times*, July 5, 2003, p. A3.

7

CULTURE

The start of the 21st century is an exciting time for Ukrainian culture. After centuries of suppression and neglect under Polish, Russian, and Soviet domination, the rich traditions of Ukrainian culture are being revived everywhere. Ukrainian language classes across the country are filled with eager students. Ukrainian folklore, folk art, and folk music are more popular than ever. National plays and operas are performed frequently. The Ukrainian people are celebrating their heritage as they seek a national identity denied them for much of their history.

However, separating what is Ukrainian from what is Russian in this culture is not always easy. For many years, Ukrainian writers, artists, and composers were identified as Russian, and some are still so today. Yet many of these creative artists remained Ukrainian in their bold styles and unique perspectives. As the Ukrainian cosmonauts have conquered space (see chapter 8), these artists have often been pioneers in exploring new styles and ways of expressing themselves.

Language

Ukrainian is one of the East Slavic languages and is, not surprisingly, very similar to Russian. For centuries, Russian was the official language of the country, but the Russians could no more stamp out the Ukrainian language than they could the spirit of the people who continued to speak it. In 1990, Ukrainian was declared the nation's official language.

Place-names, including street signs, throughout the country have been changed from Russian to Ukrainian. For example, the capital city is no longer the Russian *Kiev* but the Ukrainian *Kyiv*. Ukrainian became the primary language of instruction in all schools. However, Russian is still widely spoken in many parts of the country. The Ukrainian government has worked tirelessly since independence to promote Ukrainian, providing language classes for those rusty in its use. Many people speak both Russian and Ukrainian.

Literature

East Slavic literature, as with much of Slavic culture, was born in Kyivan Rus. Great works of religion, history, and epic tales make up the bulk of the earliest writings. The oldest literary classic, dating back to the 10th century, is the *Tales of Bygone Years*, the definitive chronicle of early Ukrainian history. There is also Abbot Danylo's vivid description of his two-year journey to the Holy Land in 1106 and the epic *Lay of Igor's Campaign*, written about the same time.

The Mongol invasion in the 1200s abruptly halted the flowering of Ukrainian literature for several centuries. The oral tradition, however, persisted where the printed word disappeared. The Kozaks in the 16th century created their own literary tradition with heroic songs of their exploits called *dumy*. The same century saw the first printing presses in Ukraine and the first printed books, including the Gospels of the New Testament and a dictionary. While these first books were written in Ukrainian, later works were mostly written in Russian, the language of Ukraine's new masters.

By the 19th century, such great Ukrainian writers as Nikolai Gogol (1809–52), Anton Chekhov (1860–1904), and Fyodor Dostoevsky (1821–81), who was half Ukrainian, were identified as Russian writers and still are by most people today. Other famous writers born in Ukraine include novelist Joseph Conrad (1857–1924), who wrote in English, Yiddish storyteller Sholem Aleichem (1859–1916), and Jewish novelist Yosef Agnon (1888–1970) who won the Nobel Prize in literature in 1966.

Gogol celebrated his Ukrainian ancestry in his short novel *Taras Bulba* (1835), which takes place during the fierce war between Kozaks and Poles in the 17th century. It is the tragic story of the Kozak leader Taras Bulba, who is betrayed by a son who falls in love with a Polish girl. Interestingly, Gogol's own ancestor, Kozak Ostop Gogol, went over to the Polish side during this same turbulent period. In the novel's climax, Taras faces death bravely at the hands of the Poles as he watches his men escape:

> From his lofty post of observation he could see everything, as in the palm of his hand.
>
> "Take possession, my lads, take possession quickly," he shouted, "of the hillock behind the forest: they can't approach it!" But the wind did not carry his words to them. "They'll perish, perish for nothing!" he said, in despair, and glanced down to where the Dnyeper [Dnipro] gleamed. Joy shone in his eyes. He described the sterns of four boats peeping out from behind the bushes; and he gathered together all the strength of his voice, and shouted in a ringing tone: "To the shore, to the shore, my lads! descend the path on the left, under the cliff. There are boats on the strand; seize them all, that the foe may not catch you!"
>
> This time the breeze blew from the other quarter, and all his words were audible to the kazaks [Kozaks]. But for this counsel he received a blow on the head with the butt-end of an axe, which made everything dance before his eyes. . . .
>
> When Taras Bulba recovered from the blow, and glanced at the Dnyeper, the kazaks were already in the skiffs, and were rowing away. Bullets showered upon them from above, but did not reach them. And the old Ataman's eyes sparkled with joy.
>
> "Farewell, comrades!" he shouted to them from above; "remember me, and come hither again next spring to make merry!—What if ye have captured me, ye devilish Lyakhs? Think ye that there is anything in the world which the kazak fears?"

The most prominent and influential Ukrainian writer of the 19th century was Taras Shevchenko (1814–61). Shevchenko was born a serf and, after being orphaned, was brutally abused as a child by a church caretaker who adopted him. He apprenticed himself to mural painters and

LESYA UKRAYINKA (1871–1913)

The life of this great Ukrainian writer is a study in determination and courage. She was born Larisa Kvita-Kosach, into a family of intellectuals. Her mother was a well-known writer and her father a prominent patron of the arts. At the age of 10, she was stricken with tuberculosis and spent much of her adult life traveling the globe in search of a cure.

Kvita-Kosach began writing poetry at the age of nine. Her first volume of poems, *On the Wings of Songs* (1893), was highly praised by critics. By the time her third book of poetry appeared in 1902, she was regarded as the leading Ukrainian poet of her generation.

Despite all her traveling, Kvita-Kosach never forgot her homeland and even modified it as her pseudonym, Ukrayinka. Her passion for Ukraine did not, however, limit her scope as a writer. She was the first Ukrainian playwright to set her works in other places and times, including the Middle Ages, biblical times, and colonial America. On another level, though, most of her plays dealt with problems and issues facing the men and women of her country. She was also a prolific translator, producing Ukrainian versions of everything from the plays of Shakespeare to Egyptian folk songs.

Ukrayinka's writings expressed feelings and emotions that helped fuel the fight for Ukrainian independence, even though she herself did not live long enough to see it.

Lesya Ukrayinka is one of Ukraine's most revered modern writers. This statue of her by Mychajlo Chereshniovsky was erected in Toronto in 1975 by the Ukrainian Canadian Women's Committee. (Courtesy The Ukrainian Academy of Arts and Sciences in the U.S.A.)

exhibited a gift for painting. A group of intellectuals were so impressed with his talent that they paid for his freedom. Later, Shevchenko joined a nationalist organization and begin writing powerful tracts condemning the Russian regime and urging Ukrainian independence. For these works he was exiled to Central Asia for 10 years. There in lonely isolation, romantic poetry and novels poured out of the writer. Ironically, Shevchenko, the champion of freedom, died a week before the czar emancipated all serfs. His work continued to inspire Ukrainian writers and artists for decades.

Shevchenko's legacy lived on in the works of two writers—Ivan Franko (1856–1916) and Lesya Ukrayinka (see boxed biography). Franko was one of Ukraine's most celebrated and prolific writers. His harsh, realistic novels such as *Boa Constrictor* (1878), vividly depicted the plight of Ukrainian workers and peasants under Russian rule. Franko's published works number more than 1,000 and include poetry, plays, histories, and criticism.

Ukrayinka spent years in voluntary exile, recuperating from tuberculosis. Her poems and plays are noted for their sublime lyricism and use of Ukrainian folklore and mythology.

Both these writers died before the Soviet takeover, a fate that destroyed the careers of many writers who followed them. During the brutal Stalin years, many writers were killed, imprisoned, or deported.

Despite the fact that they might never return home, exiled writers clung to their national identity. In the 1950s, emigrés in the United States formed the Ukrainian Writers' Association in Exile, or Slavo.

Meanwhile, back in Ukraine, many writers secretly shared manuscripts, which they read and discussed. Many of these works were later smuggled out of the Soviet Union and published in Western countries.

During the 1960s, there was a thaw in Soviet repression, and writers were given more freedom to express themselves. Most prominent in this period were the so-called Writers of the Sixties, who included poets Vasyl Stus (1938–85) and Line Kostenko (b. 1930). When the thaw ended and the Soviets once more cracked down on writers, Stus was sent to a labor camp in Russia. In 1985, he was nominated as a candidate for the 1986 Nobel Prize in literature. He died later that year, at age 47, in the labor camp.

Since independence, Ukrainian literature is once again flourishing. Poetry continues to be among the most popular literary genres, and among the best-known poets are Ihor Kalynets (b. 1939) and his wife, Iryna Staslv-Kalynets (b. 1940). Both of them were imprisoned and exiled for their politically outspoken writings by the Soviets in the 1970s.

Music

When most people think of Ukrainian music, they picture a robust male chorus singing folk songs or colorfully dressed folk dancers leaping into the air doing the athletic dance called the *hopak*, meaning "grasshopper" in English. The dance originated from exercises that prepared the Kozaks for fighting in battle.

The Ukrainian National Chorus poses for a group picture in the early 20th century. Folk singing has a long and honored tradition in Ukraine. (Courtesy Free Library of Philadelphia)

The folk music of Ukraine goes back to Kozak times and earlier. Many songs and ballads are traditionally sung a cappella, without accompaniment. Others are accompanied by the national instrument, the *bandura*, a large stringed folk instrument that resembles a lute.

There is also a long tradition of classical music in Ukraine. Mykola Lysenko (1842–1912) is known as the father of Ukrainian national music. He composed symphonic works that incorporated native folk tunes. Nationalistic operas, such as *A Kozak Beyond the Danube* (1863) by composer Semen Hulak-Artemovsky (1813–73), continue to be performed today. The most prominent contemporary composer is Myroslav Skoryk (b. 1938), known for his classical compositions and his film scores, which include the music for the classic film *Shadows of Forgotten Ancestors* (1964).

The Kyiv Chamber Choir, founded in 1990, specializes in both ancient and modern liturgical works. When the 20-voice choir sang at New York's Carnegie Hall in 1997, one reviewer praised their "disciplined, well-blended sound that was appealingly varied in color. . . ." Ukraine has six opera houses, nine symphony orchestras, and seven chamber orchestras.

Jazz and rock music are also popular. Among the leading popular-musical groups in Ukraine are the punk band Plach Yeremiyi and the rock group Vopli Vidoplyasova, also known as VV, who have toured the United States and other countries. Top solo musical artists include pop star Iryna Bilyk and folk songwriter and singer Nina Matvienko.

Art and Architecture

Ukrainian architecture was the glory of Kyivan Rus in its golden age. Ornate churches made of wood with towering spires, brilliant mosaics, and ornate carvings are today preserved as museums, although some of the finest churches were torn down by the Soviets in their campaign to quash Ukrainian nationalism. One church, the Cathedral of St. Sophia in Kyiv, was saved from such a fate only by the protest of many nations.

Icon painting was a dominant art form for centuries in Ukraine. These religious paintings, made with egg tempera on wooden panels, were so beautiful that they were once thought to have miraculous powers.

By the 17th century, the influence of Western Europe led Ukrainian artists to turn to such forms as sculpture and portrait painting. Taras Shevchenko created a school of realism that flourished in the 19th century. The early 20th century saw a number of powerful expressionistic artists who captured in their art the stark tragedy of their homeland in modern times.

But the most influential and important Ukrainian artist of the 20th century was sculptor Oleksandr Arkhypenko (1887–1964), known in Russian as Alexander Archipenko. Arkhypenko was born in Kyiv and moved to Paris as a young man to pursue his art. He took the technique of cubist painting, which turned everyday objects and people into geometric shapes, and brilliantly adapted it to sculpture. He moved to the United States in 1923 with his wife, at that time speaking only a few words of English.

"America fires my imagination more than any other country," Arkhypenko said soon after his arrival, "and embodies more of that flexibility, that yeastiness, which means life and vitality and movement." Arkhypenko's sculptures have all three of these qualities and can be seen today in many American museums. He was as great a teacher as he was an artist and founded his own art school. Among leading contemporary Ukrainian artists are sculptor Yevhen Prokopov and landscape and genre painter Volodymyr Podlessky (b. 1960).

Folk Arts

Folk art holds a special place in Ukrainian culture. Even the most humble wooden dwelling is adorned with elaborate carvings on the doors and windows. In previous decades, every peasant home proudly displayed at least one icon. Elaborate, colorful cross-stitching adorns everything from folk costumes to tablecloths.

Perhaps the most honored folk art is *pysanky*, the art of painting colored Easter eggs by using melted wax and dyes. Images painted on the eggs have symbolic meanings. Trees, for example, represent long life, and birds, fertility. Other images may stand for the creator's life and profession. Some Ukrainian Easter eggs are so exquisitely designed that they are family heirlooms, passed down from generation to generation.

Famed Ukrainian Easter egg artist Galina Ivanets uses a writing pin to put the finishing touches on a creation in her Kyvian workshop. Pysanky, *the art of painting Easter eggs, has experienced a revival in post-Soviet Ukraine.* (AP Photo/Efrem Lukatsky)

Theater

The theater came rather late to Ukraine, but it quickly became a popular art form. Historical dramas and puppet plays flourished in the 17th and 18th centuries. Actor-playwright Marko Kropyvorytsky (1840–1910) established the first permanent theatrical troupe in the late 1800s. His troupe traveled from town to town performing historical dramas that featured flawless heroes, beautiful heroines, and snarling villains. More mature dramas were written in the early 20th century by Ivan Franko, for whom a famous Kyiv theater is named, and Lesya Ukrayinka, who specialized in poetic drama.

After World War I and independence in 1918, Ukraine experienced a flowering of theater, led by Les Kurbas (1887–1942), who founded the Berezil Theater, and his protégé, playwright Mykola Kulish (1892–1942). Kulish's expressionistic plays were seen as ugly by authorities, and many were banned. Kurbas was killed in a Stalinist purge, and Kulish was arrested and sent into exile. It was the end of meaningful theater for many years. Nevertheless, some playwrights managed to circumvent the Soviet censors. Among them was Oleksandr Levada (b. 1909), whose space-age version of the Faust legend was produced in 1960.

OLEKSANDR DOVZHENKO (1894–1956)

Until he was 32, the greatest of Ukrainian filmmakers never set foot in a film studio or, for that matter, never saw more than a few films. "You could say that I stood a naked man on the Black Sea coast," Oleksandr Dovzhenko later wrote about his arrival at the Odesa Film Studio. "In the thirty-third year of my life I had to start learning all over again."

But then Dovzhenko had been facing challenges all his life. He was born in abject poverty in the town

Oleksandr Dovzhenko came from a peasant family, and the folkways and lyric beauty of the Ukrainian countryside infuse his films, which are among the greatest in early Soviet cinema. (Courtesy The Ukrainian Academy of Arts and Sciences in the U.S.A.)

Today the theater is alive and well in postcommunist Ukraine, with 60 professional theaters performing regularly. There are also elaborate puppet theaters in every major city.

Film

If you should go to a movie theater in Ukraine, be forewarned. There is no eating popcorn during the movie, and talking is strictly forbidden. Ukrainians love the cinema, but they are terribly serious about movies, and for good reason.

The Soviet cinema was one of the most original in the world in the 1920s, and Kyiv was a center of filmmaking. Ukrainian Oleksandr Dovzhenko (see boxed biography) was one of the greatest filmmakers of of Sosnitsa, where his father was an illiterate peasant farmer who could barely make a living. Of the family's 14 children, only Dovzhenko and a sister survived to adulthood. She became a doctor, and he, a science teacher at age 19. He soon became involved in politics and worked in foreign embassies for the Soviet government before returning to Kyiv as a cartoonist and book illustrator.

Two years after arriving at the Odesa studio, he directed his first film masterpiece, *Zvenigora* (1928). As with all his great films, it had little plot but incredible atmosphere and feeling derived from the history and folklore of his native Ukraine.

But despite his artistic triumphs, Dovzhenko was attacked by Soviet critics for making eccentric and indulgent films. Disillusioned with the impossible working conditions the government imposed on him, he turned increasingly away from films and spent his time writing short stories and novels.

During World War II, Dovzhenko worked as a war correspondent and witnessed the destruction of his beloved Ukraine. He wrote a film scenario, *Ukraine in Flames,* that Stalin disapproved of. The Soviet dictator was furious with Dovzhenko's nationalism and had him fired from the Kyiv Studio.

Disillusioned and bitter, Dovzhenko died at age 62 of a heart attack. He never lived to film his dream project, a movie of Nikolai Gogol's Kozak novel, *Taras Bulba.*

this era. Dovzhenko's early silent films, including *Zvenigora*, *Arsenal*, and *Earth*, are intensively lyrical and express the director's deep love for his homeland and its peasants.

Dovzhenko's passion for Ukrainian folklore and legend lived on in the work of Georgian-born Sergei Paradzhanov (1924–90), whose *Shadows of Forgotten Ancestors* (1964) was an international success. But Paradzhanov's career followed the tragic formula of too many Ukrainian creative artists under the Soviet regime. He was imprisoned in the 1970s on questionable charges of "homosexuality and illegal trafficking in religious icons." Released in the 1980s, Paradzhanov completed only two more films before dying of cancer.

Since independence, the Ukrainian film industry has slowly found itself. *A Friend of the Deceased* (1997), an absurdist comedy set in postcommunist Kyiv and directed by Viatcheslav Kishtofovitch (b. 1947), was nominated for an Academy Award. Yuri Illienko (b. 1936), the cameraman on *Shadows of Forgotten Ancestors*, directed the first big-budget film made in Ukraine since independence, the historical epic *A Prayer for Hetman Mazepa* (2002), about the life of a famous 17th-century Kozak leader.

A disruptive economy and the loss of the state support enjoyed under the Soviet system has made it difficult for many creative artists in Ukraine to get financial backing for their work. But artists, writers, and composers continue to keep alive traditions that draw heavily on both a rich folk heritage and the individual spirit of its creators.

NOTES

p. 67 "'From his lofty post of observation . . .'" Nikolai Gogol, *Taras Bulba: A Tale of the Cossacks* (New York: Knopf, 1931), pp. 282–284.

p. 71 "'disciplined, well-blended sound . . .'" *New York Times*, December 23, 1997, p. E5.

p. 72 "'America fires my imagination . . .'" Donald H. Karshan, editor, *Archipenko: International Visionary* (Washington, D.C.: Smithsonian Institution Press, 1969), p. 103.

p. 74 "'You could say that I stood . . .'" John Wakeman, editor, *World Film Directors*, *Vol. 1 (1890–1945)* (New York: H. W. Wilson, 1987), p. 261.

p. 75 "'homosexuality and illegal trafficking . . .'" The Internet Movie Database. Available online. URL: http://www.imdb.com/namc/nm0660886/bio, downloaded December 11, 2003.

8

DAILY LIFE

For all the promise of this potentially wealthy republic, life in Ukraine today is difficult for the vast majority of its citizens. Wages are low (averaging $40 a month), inflation is high, crime is rampant, and the government is riddled with corruption.

The hope for Ukraine, as with most nations, lies in the next generation that will one day run the country, hopefully better than their elders have. Education is the key for today's youth, and Ukraine's educational system is one of the best in Eastern Europe.

Education

Education has a long and revered history in Ukraine. It was one of the first countries in Europe to educate girls as well as boys, although only the nobility in early times sent its children to school. The Mongols ended national education, while the Poles later replaced Ukrainian schools with Catholic schools run by Jesuits. Metropolitan Petro Mohyla (1596–1647), the great Orthodox religious leader, founded the Kyiv-Mohyla Academy in 1633. This innovative institution of higher learning was open to young scholars from all classes, something unheard of in Europe at the time. Mohyla also encouraged young people to study abroad as part of their education, another new concept in learning.

The Russians shut down the Kyiv-Mohyla Academy in 1817, and it became a seminary for Russian Orthodox priests. New universities were thoroughly "Russified." The Ukrainian language was forbidden to be spoken, and Ukrainian culture was forbidden to be taught.

When the Soviets took over, education became compulsory for all youth. Also, universities and other institutes of higher learning were free to any student who qualified. But what Ukrainians were learning in the classroom was often controlled and twisted. The great Academy of Science of Ukraine, founded in 1918 under the Ukrainian republic, was corrupted by Communist doctrine and became largely a tool of the Soviets. However, important strides were made in certain scientific fields such as space exploration.

One positive legacy left by the Soviet era is universal education. In 2001, the government increased the number of years a child must attend school from eight to 12; or from ages six to 17. Upon finishing the secondary school students may apply to one of Ukraine's nine universities; special-interest colleges for careers in agriculture, music, and other fields; or one of the country's many technical colleges.

Education is a top priority in today's Ukraine. All children must attend school for 12 years. (Courtesy NATO)

While most schools are still operated by the state, a number of private schools have appeared since the early 1990s. Unfortunately, many state colleges and universities now charge tuition, which many Ukrainian families cannot afford.

In 1992, the National University of Kyiv-Mohyla Academy (KMA) reopened, more than 175 years after the Russians closed the original academy's doors. It is the first privately run university in Ukraine. In December 2002, KMA and Northwestern University Center for Technology and Innovation Management (CTM) in Chicago announced a unique partnership program. The two schools, as part of an ongoing sister cities project, will participate in joint research programs and innovation management consulting projects. Northwestern faculty are also helping to develop and teach graduate business programs at KMA. And so a great educational tradition continues into the 21st century.

Science and Technology

Ukraine has been in the forefront of scientific development and research for decades. Sergey Korolev (1906–66), a Ukrainian rocket engineer, guided the Soviet space program in its first golden decade and helped make Soviet cosmonaut Yuri Gagarin the first human in space in 1961. Ukrainian scientists and cosmonauts have continued Korolev's legacy. Ukrainian cosmonaut Leonid Kadenyuk (b. 1951) was a member of the space shuttle *Columbia* crew in 1997. During his 15-day flight, Kadenyuk conducted experiments on how a weightless environment affects physical processes.

If life on other planets exists, the first signs may come from Ukraine. In 2003, Team Encounter, a Houston, Texas, company, erected a 230-foot (70-m) diameter radio astronomy dish in Evpatoriya, Ukraine, that is beaming a digital message into space. The message includes text, photographs, and visual clips and will have reached the farthest known star in the universe in 14 years.

Ukrainian scientists are investigating the world's oceans as well as outer space. Research ships stationed in Odesa and Sevastopol study marine biology and conduct experiments in the desalinization of seawater.

Communications and Media

Since independence, Ukraine has been in a hurry to raise its communications systems to international standards. The telephone service has been completely overhauled from the dismal Soviet days, and mobile cellular phone use is growing at an impressive rate with 2 million mobile phones in use in 2001. Internet use is also increasing rapidly with 750,000 users online in 2001 using 260 Internet service providers (ISPs).

There were 289 FM radio stations and 134 AM stations in 1998. There were more than 33 television stations broadcasting in Ukraine in 1997. Viewers in eastern Ukraine also receive Russian television, and those in the western regions, Polish, Hungarian, and Slovak television.

Ukrainians may rely on the news they receive from abroad more than from their own media. Suppression and persecution of Ukrainian journalists and broadcasters under the Kuchma government have been notorious and have seriously damaged the country's international standing. Since the murder of journalist Georgy Gongadze in 2000, several other people in the media have been killed. A television station director was found beaten to death in the Donetsk region in 2001. Sergei Naboha, a popular journalist for Radio Liberty, a station funded by the United States, was found dead in a hotel room in the city of Vinnytsia in January 2003. This troubling trend will end only if a new, more democratic government that supports a free media comes to power in 2004.

Women's Roles

While many young women can receive a good education in Ukraine, their chances of finding a decent job after graduation are slim. As in Russia and other former Soviet republics, women are often the first to be fired in layoffs and job cutbacks. Two-thirds of all unemployed people in Ukraine are women. Those women who are professionals, such as teachers and doctors, are poorly paid even by Eastern European standards.

Yet at the same time, Ukrainian women, especially in the rural areas, have more freedom than ever before to live as they choose. "Girls now have few opportunities yet great freedom . . ." said Olga Shved, who runs a center in Kyiv dedicated to combating the illegal trafficking of women in Eastern Europe. "Here the towns are dying. What jobs there are go to men. So they leave."

Up to 85 percent of Ukrainian women who work as prostitutes abroad are forced into it against their will, according to Nina Karpacheva, deputy leader of the Ukrainian Parliament's Commission on Human Rights. Many go to Israel, Turkey, or Germany, lured by advertisements for high-paying jobs. Most of these ads are fronts for the growing international sex trade.

In 1996, Lena, a high school–educated 18-year-old from a Ukrainian village, answered a newspaper ad and applied for a good-paying job as an orange picker in Cyprus. The agency who paid for her airfare, however, sent her to Turkey instead, where she was forced to work as a prostitute in a hotel for nine months before finally managing to escape with the help of the Ukrainian embassy.

Other women seem more resigned to their new lives. Tamara, a 19-year-old Ukrainian, works in a massage parlor in Tel Aviv, Israel. She admits, "I'm not sure I would go back now if I could. What would I do there, stand on a bread line or work in a factory for no wages?" Until economic conditions improve and women can see a future for themselves in Ukraine, they will continue to emigrate, many to be victimized in other countries.

Sports and Recreation

For decades, Ukraine has turned out some of the finest athletes in the world, but few people realized it. In the Olympic Games and other international competitions, Ukrainian athletes competed under the banner of the Soviet Union. Not anymore. Ukraine now takes great national pride in its Olympic champions. Among its gold-medal winners are figure skaters Viktor Petrenko and Oksana Baiul (see boxed biography) and gymnast Lelia Podkopaayeva, who won two gold medals at the 1996 Summer Games in Atlanta, Georgia. She was the first woman gymnast to hold all-around champion title in European, World, and Olympic competition.

Ukrainian athletes won 23 medals at the 2000 Summer Games in Sydney, Australia, including two gold medals by swimmer Yana Klochkova (b. 1982). Among the top contenders for medals at the 2004

OKSANA BAIUL (b. 1978)

In many ways, she is the Cinderella of figure skating, but the happy ending to her fairy-tale life is still in question. Oksana Baiul was born in a grim Ukrainian factory town. When she was two, her parents divorced, and her father left. Her mother encouraged her ice skating but died of cancer when Baiul was 13. The next year, Baiul's skating coach moved to Canada without telling her. Angry and bitter, Baiul

After several difficult years, 1994 Olympic gold medal winner Oksana Baiul returned to skating in 1998 as a professional performer. (Courtesy Heinz Kluetmeier/IMG)

Games in Athens, Greece, are swimmer Andrei Serdinov and the women's gymnastics team.

Other top athletes with international reputations include runner Zhanna Pintusevich-Block (b. 1972), world-record-holding pole-vaulter Sergey Bubka (b. 1963), hockey player Dimitri Khristich (b. 1969), and tennis players Andrei Medvedev (b. 1974) and Elena Tatarkova (b. 1976). Ukrainian minister of sports Alexander Volkov (b. 1964) is a former professional basketball player with the Atlanta Hawks of the U.S. National Basketball Association (NBA).

The number-one sport in Ukraine, both professionally and among amateurs, is soccer. There are 16 professional teams, two of them in Kyiv.

threw her skates in the trash and vowed she would never skate again. Fortunately, she did not keep that promise.

Skating on her own, Baiul met the great Ukrainian skating coach Galina Zmiuoskaya. Zmiuoskaya agreed to become her coach and invited the orphan girl to move into her home. Here, Baiul found a loving family in Zmiuoskaya's daughter and son-in-law, skater Viktor Petrenko, who became a big brother to her.

Baiul's career took off. At 15, she won the world figure skating title. The next year, 1994, she skated at the Winter Olympics at Lillehammer, Norway, and won the gold.

But her career spun out of control after Lillehammer. She moved to the United States with her coach and then bought a large house in Connecticut. As she blossomed into a full-grown teenager, her changing body made her jumps more difficult. Injuries to her knee and back kept her off the ice. Then in January 1996, she was injured in a car accident and charged with drunken and reckless driving.

Since then, Baiul has worked hard to turn around her life. She published two books in 1997, one of them an autobiography for children. In 1998, she completed a rehab program and returned to skating as a cast member of the nationally touring Champions on Ice show. She is engaged to be married to a fellow Ukrainian living in the United States. "I don't want people to think of me as the Olympic Champion girl," she said in an interview. "I want them to remember me for my artistry."

The most celebrated soccer team is the former world and European champions, the Dynamo Kyiv team. Star Dynamo player Andrei Shevchenko (b. 1976) currently plays soccer with AC Milan, a top Italian soccer team.

Among board games, none is as popular as chess, which has been played by Ukrainians for more than a thousand years. Pigeon-raising is another favorite pastime, along with gardening and the making of folk music instruments.

When Ukrainians want to get away from the bustle of city life, they head for the countryside or the shore. The most popular vacation destination within Ukraine is the Crimea, known for its sunny beaches and relaxing resorts. Ukrainians who can afford a vacation abroad tend to go to Turkey and Eastern European countries, where the prices are reasonable. An inexpensive form of recreation is a day at the circus. Circuses can be found in every major city and are housed in beautiful permanent buildings. The Kyiv Circus even has a school where students train for several years to become clowns and other circus performers.

Food and Drink

Another favorite Ukrainian pastime is eating. Whether enjoying a meal at home or in a cozy restaurant, Ukrainians turn eating into a memorable experience that often takes hours.

Bread is the mainstay of the Ukrainian diet, and it comes in a multitude of tantalizing varieties. There is a special kind of bread for every festive occasion. *Babka* is a rich, sweet bread shaped like a woman in a dress (hence its name) and is eaten at Christmas and Easter. *Palianytsia* is ring shaped and a special treat at weddings. *Paska* is shaped like a cross and is eaten at Easter time.

Soups are also popular. *Borchuch*, also known as borscht, is a beet-cabbage soup that is a national favorite. Although it is also popular in Russia, Poland, and other Slavic countries, Ukrainians will tell you flatly that *borchuch* was first made in their country. In addition to the beets that give it its red color, *borchuch* can contain more than a dozen different vegetables and grains. It is served hot in the winter and cold in the summer.

Varenyky, dough dumplings, is the national dish. They can be served as an appetizer, main course, or dessert, depending on the filling, which varies from meat and fish to vegetables and fruits.

Ukrainian food is highly seasoned and often pickled to preserve it through the long winter. Pickled foods include cucumbers, tomatoes, mushrooms, and even fruits such as apples.

One Ukrainian specialty that is enjoyed the world over is *kotleta po kievski*. It is a breaded chicken breast flattened and rolled around a seasoned stick of butter and then fried to tenderness. It is better known to non-Ukrainians as chicken Kiev.

Among beverages, tea is more popular than coffee, and vodka is the preferred alcoholic drink. It is usually served very cold in tiny glasses.

Holidays

Holidays are a time to celebrate the rich traditions of the past and to forget the troubles of the present. A Ukrainian Christmas is unlike Christmas anywhere else. For one thing, the holiday is celebrated on January 7 instead of December 25. The Orthodox Church follows the old Julian calendar, which is 13 days behind the newer Gregorian calendar.

"Old Christmas," as it is called, begins on Christmas Eve with candles placed in the windows of each home to guide the Holy Family there. Children go from home to home singing traditional Christmas songs, called *kolyodhy*, in exchange for candy or a small gift of money. The custom is an interesting blending of Western Christmas caroling and Halloween trick-or-treating. The Christmas Eve banquet consist of 12 meatless and milkless dishes, one for each of Christ's 12 apostles. To re-create the manger in Bethlehem where Jesus was born, hay is placed on the floor of each home and pets or farm animals are brought into the house, to the delight of the children.

Ukrainian Easter is even more festive than Christmas. It usually lasts from Easter Sunday through the following Thursday. *Pysanky* eggs are made, blessed by priests, and given as gifts. People visit friends and relatives, dress up in national folk costumes, and sing and dance at special Easter festivals.

A more contemporary holiday that is close to the hearts of Ukrainians is International Women's Day on March 8. Families honor their mothers, wives, and sisters with gifts of flowers and a dinner at a restaurant, a special treat. Independence Day celebrated on August 24, commemorates when Ukraine proclaimed its independence from the Soviet Union in 1991 with parades and fireworks displays.

NOTES

pp. 80–81 "'Girls now have few opportunities . . .'" *New York Times*, January 11, 1998, p. A6.

p. 81 "'I'm not sure I would go back . . .'" *New York Times*, January 11, 1998, p. A6.

p. 83 "'I don't want people to think . . .'" "Oksana Then and Now," View Zone, available online, URL: http://www.viewzone.com/oksana22.html, downloaded December 11, 2003.

9

CITIES

Ukraine is a highly urbanized nation. About 71 percent of its people live in or near cities. These cities of Ukraine are the cultural, social, and economic nerve centers of the nation. Each metropolis exudes a personality all its own, but they all share some common characteristics: a restless energy, a cultural richness, and a colorful past.

Glorious Kyiv

"All roads lead to Kyiv," goes an old Ukrainian saying. For both Ukrainians and Russians, this is no exaggeration. For centuries, Kyiv (pop. 2,588,400)* was as much the center of the eastern Slavic world as Rome was of the Mediterranean world. Before the rise of Kyiv, there were only wandering tribes in the region; after it, there rose a civilization that gave birth to Russia.

Today Kyiv is the capital of Ukraine, the ninth largest city in Europe, and the third largest city in the CIS; only Moscow and St. Petersburg are bigger. Like these two Russian cities, Kyiv has its own unique beauty. "To stroll off Khreshchatyk, the main street, past buildings painted in pastels and shaded by chestnuts," observed one writer, "is to feel an Old World softness that Moscow seldom matches."

---

*All populations given in this chapter are 2003 estimates.

Kyiv was settled in the 600s or earlier by Slavic peoples and within two centuries was the capital of the first Russian state. Under great men of vision such as Volodymyr the Great and Yaroslav the Wise, Kyivan Rus expanded and grew into a major commercial and cultural center.

The Mongolian invasion brought the glory to an end, reducing the city to rubble. After several centuries of Lithuanian and Polish rule, Kyiv came under Russian control again in the 1600s, but now Moscow, not Kyiv, was in command of this new empire. By 1800, the city was a far cry from its past grandeur, made up of a collection of three village-like settlements. One visitor at the time declared that "Kiev hardly deserves to be called a city at all."

Yet from a population of 20,000 in 1800, Kyiv steadily grew to 70,000 by 1870, the year the railroad connected it with Moscow and Odesa on the Black Sea. This growth continued into the 20th century. World War II nearly destroyed Kyiv, but a strenuous rebuilding program after the war brought back much of its greatness. Another rebirth has been going on since independence in 1991. Some of the signs and symbols of the communist era were torn down. Streets and squares were renamed. Churches were converted from museums back into places of worship.

Once called the "golden-domed city" because of the gold leaf–covered cupolas of its many churches, today Kyiv is once again a city of churches. There are some 400 of them, the finest being St. Sophia Cathedral. It is one of the few great works of the city's medieval period that escaped destruction during World War II. Named for the celebrated church in Byzantium after which it was modeled, St. Sophia was begun in the 11th century and took 700 years to complete.

The city's other great medieval landmark is the Monastery of the Caves. It consists of two subterranean systems of sandstone tunnels that contain the burial grounds of many famous Ukrainians, whose bodies have been miraculously preserved through the cool temperatures and good soil. Among the celebrated dead is the monk Nestor (ca. 1056–1113), Ukraine's first historian.

Much of Kyiv today is a modern, well-planned city, with broad boulevards and green parks. Most residents live in vast rows of apartment houses that surround the city. They work in factories and plants that produce a myriad of products, from chemicals to cameras to heavy machinery.

The old and new meld together in Kyiv's Independence Square, where a statue of the archangel Michael atop an arch is a symbolic reconstruction of the city's celebrated medieval gates. (AP Photo/Efrem Lukatsky)

Many of the old statues and monuments of the Soviet era remain in Kyiv, reflecting the reluctance of postindependence governments to break with the communist past. However, there are signs of change. The October Revolution Square, near Khreshchatyk has been renamed Independence Square. New monuments to commemorate Ukrainian nationalism and freedom have been built. Perhaps the most controversial of these is a gilded statue of "Mother Ukraine" going up in a new city square to celebrate independence from Russia. Ironically, some critics have attacked the statue as "too Soviet," while others, such as 24-year-old Roman Godysh, call it a symbol "of beauty and independence."

But independence has had its downside in Kyiv. Its suddenness did not allow for the planned establishment of social services to replace those under the Soviet system. Up to 100,000 of the city's children are consequently homeless, many of them without families. Forced to survive on their own, they often turn to crime and drug use. Where the government has failed, private citizens have stepped in to help. Jane Hyatt and Barbara Klaiber, two American expatriates, have established a children's shelter in a former sanatorium. They call it the Ark and hope to be able to house 100 children when the eight buildings of the site are renovated. While this is only a modest start in correcting an overwhelming problem, the two women hope others, including the government, will emulate their efforts.

Culturally speaking, Kyiv has numerous colleges, theaters, and a world-renowned ballet company. The Ukrainian Academy of Sciences is also located here. Among the many museums are the Kyiv Museum of Ukrainian Decorative Folk Arts and the Historical Museum of Treasures, which houses a spectacular display of precious stones, coins, and other metalwork from every period of Ukrainian history. Perhaps the most intriguing museum is the Kyiv Museum of Theatre, Music, and Cinema Arts. Most important 20th-century Ukrainian artists, actors, writers, and filmmakers are represented here by costumes, posters, manuscripts, and other memorabilia.

The spirit of independence has brought new life into one of Europe's oldest cities. The mother of all Russian cities is proud to be Ukraine's capital, basking in a colorful past but looking forward to a new and exciting future.

Kharkiv—The Boston of Ukraine

Kyiv is secure in its Ukrainian identity. Less so is Ukraine's second largest city Kharkiv (pop. 1,435,200). It is located in the easternmost part of Ukraine in the upper Donets valley, only 25 miles (40 km) from the Russian border. Russian is still spoken by 94 percent of the people of Kharkiv. The changing of street signs and other city signs to the Ukrainian language is steady but slow. For all its Ukrainian traditions, Kharkiv remains a city caught between two cultures.

Yet Kharkiv is one of the country's younger cities, and there is an energizing, enterprising spirit here that bodes well for its future. The Kharkiv Partnership is an ongoing project developed by the U.S. and Ukrainian governments. In January 2002, under its auspices, 30 companies from the Kharkiv region exhibited their wares at a mini–trade show in Carthage, Ohio. Among those businesses represented were chemical, aviation equipment, food-processing, and information technology companies. This exchange of information and expertise will, it is hoped, lead to increased trade and U.S. investment in Kharkiv. According to Jan Sherbin, whose Glasnost Communications provided translation services for the event, "There can be a lot of energy and a lot accomplished when people in the same field get together and do things cooperatively."

Founded by the Kozaks in 1656, Kharkiv served as Kozak frontier headquarters and a fortress defense for Moscow's southern border. When many Kozaks rebelled against Russia several decades later, Kharkiv remained loyal to Russia under the Ukrainian Kozaks. Because of its allegiance to Russia, Kharkiv enjoyed more freedom than other Ukrainian cities for the next two centuries. Only near the end of the 1800s did Kharkiv return to its Ukrainian roots, becoming the vital center of several intellectual and literary movements. During this time it earned the nickname "the Boston of Ukraine." In 1919, under Soviet domination, Kharkiv became the capital of the Soviet republic of Ukraine. It remained so until 1934, when the capital was moved to Kyiv.

World War II brought disaster for Kharkiv. The Germans occupied the city for nearly two years and killed 100,000 people. The Soviets rebuilt the city, filling its streets with huge government buildings and massive squares. Kharkiv's Dzherzhinsk Square is one of the largest of its kind in the world.

Kharkiv's factories manufacture aircraft, agricultural machinery, and motorcycles. But it is the city's cultural life that is most vibrant. Kharkiv University is one of Ukraine's leading institutes of higher learning, and the Kharkiv Art Museum and History Museum hold enormous collections of great art and artifacts.

Odesa by the Sea

If Kharkiv is Ukraine's Russian city, Odesa (pop. 1,022,300) is its melting pot. More than 100 nationalities call Ukraine's largest port their home, a fact in which the city takes great pride. Odesa also takes pride in its outspokenness in the face of injustice. The city's journalists and broadcasters have been in the forefront of the attack on the city and region's corrupt politicians and officials. Three leading figures in the media, including

CHERSONESOS—A TREASURED PAST

Outside of Sevastopol on the Black Sea coast lies what archaeologists are calling one of the best preserved sites of the ancient world: Chersonesos, the northernmost colony of the early Greeks. Chersonesos, which means "peninsula" in Greek, is more than one site. As archaeologists dig down, they have uncovered the ruins of one civilization after another.

"There is no place on earth like Chersonesos," noted Dr. Joseph Coleman Carter, director of the Institute of Classical Archaeology at the University of Texas. "Greek, Roman, and Byzantine all had their day. Every epoch built its way of life on this soil. . . . If we could restore what is here and present that to people, it would be remarkable."

Unfortunately, it will not be easy. The ambitious restoration will cost millions of dollars, which Ukraine can hardly afford without outside help. Secondly, the Ukrainian Orthodox Church, which owns much of the property where the ruins are located, is opposed to its development and favors destroying the pagan buildings and artifacts.

The Ukrainian Cultural Ministry and many other Ukrainians support the Chersonesos project, but the church is a power to be reckoned with. As a result of these problems, Chersonesos made the 100 most-endangered cultural sites' list of the World Monument Fund in 2002. While the controversy continues, Carter and other archaeologists continue to unearth the past's priceless treasures, from Scythian tombs to Greek farmhouses. "It's been here for thousands of years," said Leonid Marchenko, a director of a local museum. "It's all in one place. We just need to let it out."

Boris Derevianko, editor of television's popular *Odesa Evening News*, have been murdered in the past several years. To date, no one has been arrested for these crimes. On May 15, 2003, a lawyer for the Odesa Plus Independent Television Company was viciously assaulted by two unknown assailants, and documents in a court case involving the company were stolen from him.

Odesa has long been a center for nationalist defiance. It was first settled by Ottoman Turks in 1415. It was not called by its present name until the Russians took it over in the 1790s. They named it after the ancient

Greek colony of Odessos, which they erroneously believed was previously located there. The Russians transformed Odesa into a naval port and a fortress to defend the country from Europeans to the south. By the late 19th century, it was the largest city in the Ukraine and the second largest port in the Russian Empire after St. Petersburg. But it also became a center for new ideas, some of them opposed by the Russian government.

When the Revolution of 1905 broke out, Odesa's workers were on the frontlines of the rebellion. The crew of the battleship *Potemkin* mutinied in the Black Sea and found support and shelter in Odesa. This historical moment is immortalized in the 1925 silent film classic *Potemkin*. The film's climax takes place on the Maritime Stairs, 192 steps that link a main boulevard of the city with the port section. Director Sergei Eisenstein's filming of the massacre of innocent residents by the czar's Kozaks never actually took place on the steps, but the grand staircase to the sea has been renamed the "Potemkin Steps" in honor of the mutineers.

Today Odesa remains a cosmopolitan city of beaches, spas, and multiethnic communities. "Odesa has always shown more color, spirit and

Odesa is filled with historic 19th-century Russian-style architecture, such as this ornate building. (Courtesy Library of Congress)

irreverence than other cities of the former Soviet Union," point out authors Linda Hodges and George Chumak. "There's an excitement, a verve, an anything-is-possible feeling in its streets."

But even Odesa must face up to life's grim realities. While in sounder economic shape than most Ukrainian cities, when problems arise, the city has few resources to fix them. For example, the revered Odesa Opera and Ballet House, a city landmark since 1887, is in desperate need of repair. Neither the national government nor city officials have the $18 million needed for the renovations. A committee organized by the opera house's director is trying to raise the funds, but few citizens have the money to donate in these troubled economic times.

Lviv—Capital of Western Ukraine

Lviv (pop. 700,100), the major city of west Ukraine, has been called the most Ukrainian of Ukrainian cities. It is located near the Polish border in the northern foothills of the Carpathian Mountains. Ukrainian nationalism did not have to be reintroduced in Lviv because it never left. Geographically the closest part of the country to the West and the last region to come under Soviet domination, western Ukraine is home to a proud and spirited people. The people of Lviv have needed that spirit to survive the daily grind of life. Since independence, their city has suffered greatly. Although culturally independent of the Soviet Union, Lviv was economically dependent on the Soviet market for military armaments and equipment. When the Soviet Union collapsed, there was no market for many of these products. When plants and factories closed, thousands of people were put out of work. By 1999, nearly one-third of all city workers were unemployed. "How can we survive?" complained Natasha Cedovina, a young widow with a daughter. "There's nothing for gas, nothing for electricity. It is a circle without end."

Lviv's turbulent history began with its founding in 1256 by Prince Danylo Holytsky of Galicia-Volyin, a medieval kingdom south of Poland. He named it after his son Prince Lev.

Over the next 500 years, this trading center and outpost was ruled in succession by the Poles, the Turks, the Swedes, and then the Poles again. In 1772, with the first partition of Poland, it came under the domain of the Austro-Hungarian Empire. Lviv became the capital of Galicia, no longer a kingdom but a region of southeastern Poland. When the empire crumbled after World War I, Lviv became the capital of the Western Ukrainian Democratic Republic. One of the shortest-living republics to emerge from the war, it was seized by the new republic of Poland in 1919. It remained part of Poland until the Soviets annexed it in 1939.

Despite German occupation, Lviv was spared the wholesale destruction of other Ukrainian cities. The Soviets could not reach the region until the war was nearly over, and the Germans had already been vanquished. Western Ukraine was openly rebellious to Soviet rule from the start. Lviv was the focal point of a dissident movement in the 1980s that propelled the country toward independence.

Lviv's long past lives on in its famous Market Square, which dates back to 1380 and lies in the heart of the city's old town. You might not think of a cemetery as a tourist attraction, but Lviv's Lychakiv Cemetery is considered one of the most beautiful in Europe, with thousands of monuments and sculptures amid lush greenery. Among the famous Ukrainians buried there is writer Franko, for whom the city's Ivan Franko University is named.

Like Lychakiv, Lviv's beauty is sad and forlorn. "Lviv," wrote Ukrainian-American Ania Savage on a visit in 1991, "is like a once pretty woman who must contend with bad times and the accumulation of years."

Yalta—Jewel of the Crimea

Yalta (pop. 77,700), located in southern Crimea on the Black Sea, will forever be connected with the meeting of the "Big Three" Allied leaders of World War II: Prime Minister Winston Churchill of Great Britain, President Franklin Roosevelt of the United States, and Soviet leader Joseph Stalin. They met there at Livadia, former summer estate of Czar Nicholas II, in February 1945 to plan the postwar peace, a peace that was destroyed by Stalin's plan to dominate Eastern Europe.

But Yalta had a long and colorful history well before the Yalta Conference. It was founded as a Greek colony, Yalita, in the first century A.D. and was passed back and forth among invaders and conquerors for centuries. In 1783, the Russians moved in when they annexed all of Crimea from Turkey. Forty years later, a Russian prince named Vorontsove turned the modest town into a small city.

Yalta's Mediterranean climate and beautiful beaches attracted Russia's nobility, who built summer estates there for their families. During the Soviet era, Communist leaders built handsome dachas, Russian country homes, in or near Yalta. Khrushchev's dacha, later taken over by his successor, Brezhnev, was equipped with a 250-foot-deep (76 m) bomb shelter. Gorbachev's villa, 25 miles (40 km) west of Yalta, became the vacation home of Ukrainian presidents after independence.

Writers have also been attracted to Yalta's natural beauty. Writer Anton Chekhov spent his last years here, creating the plays *The Cherry Orchard* and *Three Sisters*. Today his home is a museum. There is also a theater named in Chekhov's honor. Besides tourism, Yalta's major industries are wine making and tobacco processing.

Three Industrial Giants

North of the Crimea in southeastern Ukraine lie three cities that are among the nation's industrial giants.

Dnepropetrovsk (pop. 1,025,700) is located on the mighty Dnipro River and is one of the country's major river ports. It lies in the heart of the coal-mining region known as Donbas and is the center of Ukraine's steel and iron industries. Dnepropetrovsk is also home to the world's biggest rocket and satellite plant, Yuzhmash. Rockets made at Yuzhmash carried a communications satellite into space in October 1999 from a launching platform in the Pacific Ocean. The project, called Sea Launch, was a collaborative effort of Ukraine, the United States, Russia, and Norway. For all its industry, Dnepropetrovsk has more than 3,000 acres (1,215 hectares) of parks for its citizens to enjoy.

The city was founded in 1787 by Russian general Grigori Potemkin who named it Ekaterinoslav, after his queen, Catherine the Great. It was given its current name in 1926.

A little to the south of Dnepropetrovsk, on the opposite bank of the Dnipro, sits Zaporizhzhya (pop. 783,000), site of the Dneproges hydroelectric dam and power station, one of the first and largest of its kind in the former Soviet Union. The name means "beyond the rapids." For three centuries, the city was the headquarters of the Zaporizhzhya Kozaks in their struggle against the Poles, and was a focal point of the recent independence movement.

The Dneproges Dam, rebuilt after World War II, is the city's blessing and its curse. The waste from the dam and nearby plants has seriously polluted Zaporizhzhya and the surrounding area.

Pollution has been better controlled in Donetsk (pop. 984,900) farther east on the Kalmius River. Surrounded by coal mines and steel mills, Donetsk has more park land than any other Ukrainian city. Despite its industrial reputation, it has a rich cultural life and is home to five colleges and universities, the Ukrainian Theatre of Music and Drama, and a popular puppet theater.

Industry and culture, modernity and tradition—the great cities of Ukraine have been able to balance the needs of the larger nation with the needs of the people who live and work there.

NOTES

p. 87 "'To stroll off Khreshchatyk . . .'" Mike Edwards, "Ukraine: Running on Empty," *National Geographic*, March 1993, p. 44.

p. 88 "'Kiev hardly deserves to be called . . .'" Michael F. Hamm, *Kiev: A Portrait, 1800–1917* (Princeton, N.J.: Princeton University Press, 1993), p. 21.

p. 89 "'too Soviet'" *New York Times*, January 13, 2002, p. 3.

p. 89 "'of beauty and independence,'" *New York Times*, January 13, 2002, p. 3.

p. 91 "'There can be a lot of energy . . .'" Business Courier, available online, URL: http://cincinnati.bizjournals.com/cincinnati/stories/2002/01/21/story7.html, downloaded November 3, 2003.

p. 92 "'There is no place on earth . . .'" *New York Times*, November 25, 1997, p. F1.

p. 92 "'It's been here for thousands of years . . .'" *New York Times*, November 25, 1997, p. F8.

pp. 93–94 "'Odesa has always shown . . .'" Linda Hodges and George Chumak, *Language and Travel Guide to Ukraine* (New York: Hippocrene Books, 1994), p. 289.

p. 94 "'How can we survive? . . .'" *New York Times*, February 26, 1999, p. A1.

p. 95 "'Lviv is like a once pretty woman . . .'" Ania Savage, *Return to Ukraine*. (College Station, Tex.: A & M University Press, 2000), p. 49.

10

PROBLEMS AND
SOLUTIONS

Ever since the glory days of Kyivan Rus, Ukraine has been, as its name suggests, a borderland. Like other borderlands, its history has been filled with romantic outlaws, fierce invaders, and powerful conquerors. It has often found itself in a no-man's-land—neither a republic nor a colony, neither a rich land nor a poor one, not a free nation, but refusing to be an enslaved one.

Although it has been independent since 1991, Ukraine is still dependent on others for many things, such as energy, capital, and trade. In the 21st century, Ukraine faces many problems, some of them of its own devising. These problems are soluble, but working out the solutions will not be easy. It will take as much energy, imagination, and perseverance to solve them as it did to break away from the Soviet Union.

The Soviet Factor

"It seems very strange that Ukraine . . . ever chose to become independent from us," a Russian high school teacher told an American journalist. "In the end, they won't be able to live without Russia and they'll rejoin."

Many Russians, a number of them who live in Ukraine, share this sentiment. They see Ukraine's assertion of independence as a temporary phenomenon, something that will pass, like a fever. After all, Ukraine had been a part of the Russian and Soviet empires for more than 300 years.

Most Ukrainians view the situation differently. For them, Russia is just another of the interlopers who have taken away their freedom and drained their land of its rich resources for their own use. Ukraine has as little interest in rejoining Russia as does nearly every other former Soviet republic.

Yet Ukraine still needs Russia at least as much as Russia needs it. Russia provides Ukraine with gas and oil, two natural resources of which this resource-rich country has little. Russia is still Ukraine's number-one trade partner and is likely to remain so for some time. Ukrainian farmers regularly bring their produce to Russian markets to sell, knowing that they will get a better price for their goods there than at home.

Even if the day comes when Ukraine can stand economically independent of Russia, it will still have to deal politically with its nearest

A demonstrator in an anti-Russian protest flashes the Ukrainian national emblem, a trident. The protesters are awaiting the arrival of Russian president Vladimir Putin for a summit meeting of ex-Soviet republic leaders. (AP Photo/ Viktor Pobedinsky)

neighbor. As one Ukrainian puts it, "Russia is a huge power and it will always be next to us."

After several years of difficult relations, Ukraine and Russia have forged new bonds of friendship. The issue of ownership of the Black Sea naval fleet in the Crimea has been worked out to the satisfaction of both sides and land delimitations of boundary lines have been settled. In a meeting in 2002 with President Kuchma, Russian president Putin offered to coordinate Ukraine's joining the World Trade Organization (WTO) and even offered Russian expertise and funding to complete the two nuclear reactors that will replace the closed reactors at the Chornobyl nuclear plant.

The Crimean Question

Nowhere were the tensions between Russia and postindependent Ukraine more apparent than in the Crimea. This peninsula of land extending south from Ukraine into the Black Sea wanted to be independent. Ukrainians insisted the Crimea belonged to them ever since Khrushchev gave it over to Ukraine in 1954. Ukraine feared that if Crimea became completely autonomous, it would once again become part of Russia. Indeed, many Russians hoped this would happen, as did many Crimeans: 70 percent of the population is Russian. "People think they were better off before," says a Ukrainian naval captain in the Crimea, referring back to the Soviet era. "They don't remember the bad things."

The most contested issue in the Crimea has been the powerful Black Sea fleet in Sevastopol, Crimea's capital. Russia argued the naval fleet and the city were its property. Ukraine responded that the fleet was on its sovereign territory and refused to give it up. Ukrainians felt that if Russia took over the fleet, it would use the navy to take over the entire region.

In 1997, the two nations finally signed an accord that divided the Black Sea fleet equally between them. While the Crimea remained a sovereign part of Ukraine, Russia was allowed to lease the ports around Sevastopol for 20 years for nearly $100 million per year. Russia also reduced Ukraine's $3 billion debt by $726 million for use of the fleet and the transfer of Ukraine's nuclear arsenal five years earlier.

While there is relative peace in the Crimea between Russia and Ukraine, ethnic tensions have created a new problem on the peninsula.

Crimea's native people, the Tatars, were exiled to Siberia after World War II by Stalin for supposedly collaborating with the Nazis. In the late 1980s, many Tatars began returning under the liberal policies of Soviet leader Gorbachev. Today, there are some 200,000 Tatars in the Crimea, composing about 12 percent of the population, yet the Tatars have no representation in the Crimean parliament. Many Tatars lack decent housing or jobs. Their language is not officially recognized by the local government. Lobbying groups, such as the International Committee for Crimea in Washington, D.C., have put pressure on the Ukraine government to persuade, or if necessary force, the semi-autonomous Crimean government to give Tatars their full rights as citizens. At present, the situation remains unresolved.

National Security

Despite strengthening ties with Russia, many Ukrainians consider the security of their nation to rest with Western Europe and the United States. In May 2002, the Ukrainian government began the long process of applying for NATO membership. A member of NATO's Partnership for Peace since 1994, Ukraine hopes to join the organization within the next several years. The alleged sale of arms and radar equipment to such renegade countries as Iraq under Saddam Hussein hurt Ukraine's standing with NATO countries and put its application for membership in some jeopardy. While the United States stands firm on increased human and civil rights in Ukraine, it has opened the door to negotiation. A sign that Ukraine is being seriously considered for NATO is the leasing of its jumbo military transport plane by 12 NATO members for a military deployment force. In anticipation of NATO membership, the Ukrainian parliament approved the National Security Concept, a comprehensive new plan for national security with well-defined goals and objectives.

Crime and Corruption

Crime and its links to corruption in both the public and private sector have taken a disturbing turn in Ukraine since independence. Many Ukrainians see little hope for lowering the crime rate when the government itself appears to have set itself above the law. President Kuchma's alleged involvement with the unsolved murder of journalist Georgy Gongadze and the government's underhanded attempts to control elections and the media have made Ukraine a pariah among European nations.

This sorry state of affairs and the sanctions it has led to have spurred the government to efforts to reform. In December 2002, the parliament passed new laws to tighten controls on money laundering, a major criminal activity in Ukraine. The legislation gives the government the power to examine all bank transactions over a certain amount.

In July 2003, a meeting between Kuchma and Interpol heads led to a new cooperation between Ukraine and the European crime-fighting agency, particularly in the area of money laundering and illegal immigration. The 2004 European Regional Interpol Conference was held in Ukraine.

Domestically, much more needs to be done. Local police must be better paid and trained to work more effectively to stem the wave of robbery and murder, much of it tied to organized crime families centered in Moscow and Kyiv. Other areas that need to be addressed are prostitution and illegal drug smuggling, which includes both the cultivation of cannabis and opium poppies and the international shipping of other illegal drugs from Africa, Latin America, and Turkey through Ukraine to Europe and Russia.

As for the corruption in government itself, few Ukrainians have any illusions that it will disappear with the departure of President Kuchma and his cronies. It will take a deep and concerted effort from the next president to root out the corruption that has been so deeply embedded for so long in the Ukrainian system.

Migrant Labor

While some corrupt officials and businesspeople make millions, many ordinary Ukrainians can barely make enough money to feed their families. This has led to an incredible exodus. As many as 7 million adult workers, some of them highly skilled professionals who are unemployed, have left the country for long periods to find work across Europe.

While these migrants return with as much as $1 billion to keep family members and entire villages back home alive, the cost is very high. A generation of Ukrainian children are growing up seeing their parents once a year or less. Many live with grandparents, while some are forced to live on their own.

"It is a painful dilemma," said Amy Heyden, director of the Trafficking Prevention Program at Winrock International, a preventative nonprofit organization in the United States. "On the one hand, families desperately need the income from working abroad, but it is forcing a great many children to grow up without their parents."

Although the children are at risk, so are their parents. Some find legitimate jobs, but they may have to work 18 hours a day for as little as $1.50 an hour. And these are the fortunate ones. Others are forced to work under slavelike conditions, often cheated out of much of their wages by unscrupulous employers. Because they are usually working illegally in a foreign country, they have little recourse under the law. Worst off are as many as 100,000 Ukrainian women who are trapped in lives as prostitutes in a rapidly growing sexual slavery trade.

Back home, village and town life dries up when often more than 80 percent of the working population has gone. For those left behind, usually the very old and very young, the future looks bleak. "I miss them a lot," one 10-year-old boy said about his parents, "but they have to work far away because our country is broken." Fixing these broken lives will take years, perhaps decades, as Ukraine struggles to find its way in a postcommunist world.

Health

On one hand, the state of the national health of Ukraine is considerably better than most of its neighbors, including Russia. The Ukrainians have tried to keep pace with medical technology, and the statistics support this. The mortality rate is about 21 deaths per 1,000 live births, one of the lowest among former Soviet republics.

But in other areas the health of the nation is very poor. Men's lifestyle, which typically includes heavy cigarette smoking, too much alcohol, and day-to-day stress, has shrunk the average male life expectancy to about 61 years. The average life expectancy for both sexes dropped from 71 years in 1996 to 66.5 years in 2003.

While heart disease and cancer are leading killers, the two diseases that most plague Ukraine today are acquired immunodeficiency syndrome (AIDS) and tuberculosis (TB). Ukraine has the highest rate of human immunodeficiency virus (HIV) in Eastern Europe, with about 500,000 people, or nearly 1 percent of the population, infected with the virus that eventually leads to AIDS. Part of this is due to high intravenous drug use and contaminated hypodermic needles that spread HIV.

About 700,000 Ukrainians have TB, a respiratory disease that often goes hand in hand with AIDS. People with AIDS have a weakened immune system that makes them particularly vulnerable to catching TB. In December 2003, the World Bank loaned Ukraine $60 million to fight TB and HIV. While the money helps, much more foreign aid is needed to upgrade a health care system that has been falling apart since independence.

As many as 40 percent of hospitals reuse hypodermic needles and have no hot water. Rural hospitals and clinics continually experience serious shortages of medical supplies. However, only a small number of Ukrainians enjoy even this inadequate medical treatment. According to a 2001 survey of the International Labor Office (ILO), 88 percent of Ukrainian families are unable to afford basic health care.

Chornobyl

Although it took place nearly two decades ago, the nuclear reactor explosion at the Chornobyl nuclear plant, 80 miles south (129 km) of Kyiv, continues to haunt this nation. When Reactor No. 4 exploded in the early hours of April 26, 1986, it sent into the air 10 times the amount of radioactive material that was released in the U.S. atomic bombing of Hiroshima and Nagasaki in 1945. The fallout covered a 100,000-square-mile (258,980-sq-km) area, including not only Ukraine, then still part of the Soviet Union, but also Russia, Belarus, Czechoslovakia, Hungary, Poland, France, and Italy.

Since the explosion, which took 31 lives, more than 12,500 men, women, and children have died from radiation exposure, including radiation-induced diseases such as leukemia. Chornobyl, and the 75 villages that surround it, were evacuated and remain ghost towns to this day.

Despite the real danger of another of the three remaining reactors malfunctioning, first the Soviet authorities and then the independent

Ukrainian government refused to close the facility. Their reasons were purely economic: Energy-impoverished Ukraine receives nearly half its electricity from nuclear power. Finally, after years of criticism both at home and abroad, the government shut down the Chornobyl plant for good in December 2000. New, safer reactors at existing plants at Rivne and Khmelnytsky have replaced it.

But the bitter legacy of Chornobyl continues. Ukraine, along with Russia and Belarus, have severely cut benefits to surviving victims of Chornobyl, many of whom must travel to the United States or Canada to receive medical treatment for their chronic illnesses. Some 25,000 of the evacuees of Chornobyl are still without permanent housing. Even more distressing, the cleanup of contamination that still blankets northern Ukraine and parts of Russia and Belarus has been reduced and compromised. Recent reports claim that cleanup workers may actually be spreading the contamination by dumping the radioactive waste in uncontaminated areas. Furthermore, and most frightening of all, the hastily constructed cement sarcophagus that surrounds the damaged nuclear reactor at Chornobyl is in danger of collapsing and desperately needs repair. Work on a new shell to prevent radiation leakage is scheduled to begin in 2004.

Meanwhile, the Chornobyl victims and their advocates keep the pressure on their governments. On the 17th anniversary of the disaster, in 2003, some 5,000 victims marched in downtown Kyiv to protest the government's lack of action and slashing of benefits. "The government is forgetting about us," said General Korostylev, head of an action group Chornobyl Shield. "They say it happened long ago, and it's not their responsibility anymore." Unless Ukraine and its neighbors recommit themselves to making sure Chornobyl does not happen again, its legacy will continue to haunt this nation for years to come.

The Environment

The ongoing legacy of Chornobyl is a grim one, but there are other equally serious threats to Ukraine's environment. Two of the country's major rivers, the Don and the Dnipro, are full of sewage and industrial waste, spreading their pollutants throughout the countryside. In even

Relatives place photographs of Chornobyl victims around a memorial monument in Kyiv on the eve of the 16th anniversary of the Chornobyl nuclear reactor explosion, the worst of its kind to date. (AP Photo/Efrem Lukatsky)

worse condition is the Black Sea, where pollution is so bad that 20 out of 26 species of fish found there have completely died out over the past 30 years due to a lack of oxygen and light. Instead, the sea is a breeding ground for jellyfish that thrive on fish larvae and phytoplankton that live on human waste.

A task force of environmentalists from Ukraine and five other countries that border the body of water are working tirelessly to save the Black Sea. They signed an agreement in the fall of 1996 to set up regulations for commercial fishing, shipping, and development of the coast. "If the habitats of these species can be protected and further damage avoided," says marine environmentalist Dr. Laurence Mee, "the sea may slowly recover from the bottom up . . . if we act now."

Another problem is deforestation caused by the overcutting of trees in the north and west for decades. This has led to serious soil erosion and flooding during periods of heavy rains. The worst natural disaster in the country occurred in 1998, when floods in western Ukraine caused millions of dollars' worth of property damage and left thousands of people homeless.

Ukraine, with its rich natural resources, thousand-year-old culture, and resilient, optimistic people, has the potential to be one of the major nations of Europe. It has much to overcome, but it also has much to gain. Only by facing its problems fearlessly will it fulfill that potential.

NOTES

p. 99   "'It seems very strange . . .'" *Washington Post,* January 5, 1997, p. A17. CD NewsBank.

p. 101   "'Russia is a huge power . . .'" *Washington Post,* January 5, 1997, p. A17. CD NewsBank.

p. 101   "'People think they were better off . . .'" Peter T. White, "Crimea: Pearl of a Fallen Empire," *National Geographic,* September 1994, p. 109.

p. 104   "'It is a painful dilemma . . .'" *Christian Science Monitor,* June 10, 2003, p. 7.

p. 104   "'I miss them a lot . . .'" *Christian Science Monitor,* June 10, 2003, p. 7.

p. 106   "'The government is forgetting about us . . .'" *Christian Science Monitor,* April 25, 2003, p. 8.

p. 107   "'If the habitats of these species . . .'" December 13, 1996, p. 6. CD NewsBank.

CHRONOLOGY

ca. 4000 B.C.

The Trypillians settle in present-day Ukraine and establish first communities

ca. 1000 B.C.

Nomadic warrior tribes, including the Cimmerians, migrate into area

ca. 700 B.C.

The Scythians invade Ukraine and control it for 500 years

ca. A.D. 300

The Varangians, or Rus, arrive from Scandinavia and unify the peoples under their leader, Rurik

978–1054

Yaroslav the Wise makes Kyiv one of the largest and most powerful cities in Europe

987

Volodymyr the Great converts Kyivan Rus to Christianity

1169

Kyiv, now in decline, is seized and looted by Kyiv prince Andrei Bogolyubsky, who moves the capital to Volodymyr

1223

The Mongols conquer Kyiv and control it for the next two centuries

1569

The Poles take over Kyivan Rus lands, now called Ukrainia, meaning "borderlands"

1648–49

The Kozaks, fierce warriors, led by Bohdan Khmelnytsky, rise up against the Poles and seize Kyiv

1654

The Kozaks and Russians sign the Treaty of Peruyaslav, uniting their countries against Poland

1659

The Kozaks, now aligned with the Poles, defeat the Russians at the Battle of Konotip

1666

Poland and Russia divide the Ukraine between them

1781

Kozak power is broken with the end of the hetmanate; Russia is in full control of the Ukraine

1825

The Decembrist Revolution against the Russian czar fails in St. Petersburg

1905

The Revolution of 1905 fails to overthrow the czar; Odesa is attacked by the czar's Kozaks for harboring mutineers of the battleship *Potemkin*

1917

The October Revolution overthrows the czar and sets off a civil war between Bolsheviks and anti-Bolshevik forces

1918

January 22: Ukraine declares its independence, becoming the Ukrainian National Republic

1921

The new Soviet state overthrows independent Ukraine and absorbs it. Within a year, it becomes one of the first socialist republics of the Soviet Union

1929

Soviet leader Joseph Stalin begins the collectivization of farms in Ukraine and elsewhere; millions of Ukrainians are imprisoned, executed, or forced to emigrate for resisting

1932–33

Some 7 million Ukrainians die of starvation in the worst human-caused famine in recorded history

1938

Nikita Khrushchev is appointed Communist leader in Ukraine and purges the local Communist Party in a reign of terror

1941

June: Germany invades Ukraine in a major attack on the Soviet Union during World War II; many Ukrainians collaborate with the Nazis

September 29: The Nazis murder about 35,000 Ukrainian Jews at Babi Yar, outside Kyiv

1945

The war ends in German defeat; many Ukrainians are imprisoned, exiled, or executed by the Soviets for collaborating with the Nazis

1946

A natural famine devastates Ukraine

1954
The Soviets turn the Crimea over to Ukraine as a goodwill gesture

1956
Khrushchev takes over as supreme Soviet leader

1964
Khrushchev falls from power and is replaced by Leonid Brezhnev, who is Ukrainian by birth

1982
Brezhnev dies at age 76

1985
Mikhail Gorbachev comes to power and loosens the Soviet grip on Ukrainian nationalism

1986
April 26: An explosion at a nuclear plant at Chornobyl, Ukraine, exposes 100,000 people to high levels of radiation

1989
September: The popular movement Rukh is born and calls for political change in Ukraine
November: Volodymyr Ivashko, a moderate Communist leader, comes to power

1991
August 19–21: An attempted coup in Moscow of Communist hardliners fails
August 24: The Ukrainian parliament declares independence from the Soviet Union
December 1: A national referendum on independence passes overwhelmingly; Leonid Kravchuk is elected first president of the new republic

1992

October: Leonid Kuchma is appointed prime minister

1993

September: Kuchma resigns from Kravchuk's corrupt government

1994

June: Kuchma is elected president

August: Sevastopol in Crimea declares itself a Russian city

October–November: Kuchma visits the United States and Canada, seeking financial aid for Ukraine

1995

March: The Ukrainian government ends a potential rebellion in Crimea

1996

June: A new constitution increasing the powers of the president is approved

1997

May: Russian leader Boris Yeltsin makes his first trip to Ukraine and signs a friendship treaty with President Kuchma

July: Ukraine signs a charter with NATO at a summit meeting in Madrid, paving the way for eventual membership in the organization

August: Ukraine celebrates its sixth anniversary of independence with military exercises that include American sailors and marines

1998

April: The Ukraine Communist Party wins one-quarter of the vote in national elections

August: State Statistics Committee reports in July that Ukraine experienced deflation for first time since independence, with a 2.3 percent reduction in food prices; President Kuchma celebrates his 60th birthday in the Crimea with representatives and leaders of Eastern Europe and the United States

1999

October 31: Kuchma wins a second presidential term

December: Viktor Yushchenko becomes prime minister

2000

November: The headless corpse of missing journalist Georgy Gongadze is found; Kuchma is allegedly implicated in his death

December: The three remaining active reactors at the Chornobyl nuclear plant are shut down

2001

June: John Paul II visits Ukraine for the fourth time since becoming pope

August 24: Ukraine celebrates 10 years of independence

October: Seventy-eight passengers of a Russian airliner die when it is shot down by the Ukrainian military

2002

May: Ukraine begins the process of applying for full membership in NATO

July: Some 85 people are killed during an air show in Lviv, one of the worst disasters of its kind

November: Kuchma dismisses Prime Minister Yushchenko and other members of his government; he nominates Viktor Yanukovich for prime minister

2003

February: Yushchenko, now an opposition leader, visits the United States

April 26: Some 5,000 Chornobyl survivors march in Kyiv to protest slashing of benefits and continuing dangers of the nuclear site

September: Ukraine sends 1,800 peacekeepers to U.S.-occupied Iraq to help rebuild the country

December: The World Bank loans Ukraine $60 million to fight widespread AIDS and tuberculosis. The Constitutional Court rules that Kuchma could run for a third term

2004

March: Thousands march in Kyiv to protest suspected government crackdown on the media before full presidential elections; European Parliament calls on authorities to conduct fair and democratic elections in October; representatives of Ukraine and Russia meet in Kyiv to discuss energy exports to Europe and other economic matters

July: Some 36 coal miners are killed at Krasnolymanska mine in one of the worst mining disasters in several years

FURTHER READING

NONFICTION BOOKS

Dolot, Miron. *Execution by Hunger: The Hidden Holocaust.* (New York: W. W. Norton, 1987). A gripping eyewitness account of Stalin's forced collectivization of Ukraine farms and the famine that followed.

Gosnell, Kelvin. *Belarus, Ukraine, and Moldova* (Brookfield, Conn.: Millbrook Press, 1992). A general introduction to Ukraine and two other former Soviet republics for middle-grade readers.

Hodges, Linda, and Chumak, George. *Hippocrene Language and Travel Guide to Ukraine* (New York: Hippocrene Books, 1994). Although a travel guide, this book is an excellent and concise introduction to the country and its people.

Kummer, Patricia. *Ukraine* (New York: Children's Press, 2001). A volume in the excellent Enchantment of the World series.

Lerner Publishers. *Ukraine Then and Now* (Minneapolis, Minn.: Lerner Publications, 1993). Another general introduction for middle grades, nicely designed with good pictures.

Savage, Ania. *Return to Ukraine* (College Station, Tex.: A & M University Press, 2000). The vivid, personal account of a Ukrainian-American journalist's return to her homeland in 1991.

Wilson, Andrew. *The Ukrainians: Unexpected Nation* (New Haven, Conn.: Yale University Press, 2000). Probably the best single volume on contemporary Ukraine available to date, written by a British lecturer in Ukrainian studies.

Zemliansky, Pavel. *Ukraine* (Milwaukee, Wis.: Gareth Stevens Publishing, 2002). Good, up-to-date young-adult country study.

FICTION, PLAYS, AND POETRY

Chekhov, Anton. *Four Great Plays* (Mincola, N.Y.: Dover Publications, 2004). The finest works of the greatest of Russian/Ukrainian playwrights. *The Cherry Orchard* and *Three Sisters* were written in the Crimea.

Gogol, Nikolai. *Taras Bulba*. Translated by Peter Constantine (New York: Modern Library, 2003). Tragic but rousing novel of fictional Kozak leader by a great Ukrainian writer, who wrote in Russian; first new English translation in 40 years.

Kostenko, Lina Vasylivna. *Wanderings of the Heart: Selected Poetry of Lina Kostenko* (Handen, Conn.: Garland Publishing, 1990). A generous selection of the work of one of Ukraine's leading contemporary poets.

WEBSITES

ArtUkraine.com. Available online. URL: http://www.artukraine.com/addurl.htm. A site "dedicated to the advancement of Ukrainian arts, culture, history, and heritage." It also features current events.

Kyiv Post. Available online. URL: http://www.kyivpost.com/. The website for the *Kyiv Post* weekly newspaper, Ukraine's leading English-language newspaper, and the *Kyiv Post Daily* newsletter. Some articles are free online, but users must first register to access.

Ukraine News. Available online. URL: http://www.ukrainenews.com. A comprehensive daily news magazine that features articles on Ukraine from various newspapers including the *International Herald Tribune* and Canada's *National Post*.

INDEX

Page numbers followed by *m* indicate maps, those followed by *i* indicate illustrations, and those followed by *c* indicate an item in the chronology.